The Five Keys *to* Mindful Communication

D0963146

The Five Keys *to* Mindful Communication

Using Deep Listening and Mindful Speech
to Strengthen Relationships, Heal Conflicts,
and Accomplish Your Goals

Susan Gillis Chapman

Shambhala • *Boston & London* • 2012

Shambhala Publications, Inc.
Horticultural Hall
300 Massachusetts Avenue
Boston, Massachusetts 02115
www.shambhala.com

©2012 by Susan Gillis Chapman

All rights reserved. No part of this book may be reproduced
in any form or by any means, electronic or mechanical, including
photocopying, recording, or by any information storage and retrieval
system, without permission in writing from the publisher.

9 8 7 6 5 4 3 2 1

First Edition

Printed in the United States of America

♾ This edition is printed on acid-free paper that meets the
American National Standards Institute Z39.48 Standard.
♻ This book is printed on 30% postconsumer recycled paper.
For more information please visit www.shambhala.com.

Distributed in the United States by Random House, Inc.,
and in Canada by Random House of Canada Ltd

Designed by James D. Skatges

Library of Congress Cataloging-in-Publication Data
Chapman, Susan Gillis.
The five keys to mindful communication: using deep listening
and mindful speech to strengthen relationships, heal conflicts,
and accomplish your goals / Susan Gillis Chapman.—1st ed.
p. cm.
Includes bibliographical references and index.
ISBN 978-1-59030-941-4 (pbk.: alk. paper)
1. Interpersonal communication. 2. Interpersonal conflict.
3. Awareness. I. Title.
BF637.C45C45 2012
153.6—dc23
2011035930

This book is dedicated to my parents,
Gwyneth and Jack.

And to my teachers, especially
the mothers of the Sacred Heart
and
the Sakyongs of Shambhala.

I can never repay your kindness.

Contents

Acknowledgments

This book is the result of the inspiration and input from many people over a twelve year period. Liz Dodd and Pennelope Goforth and other friends in Juneau helped get the project started after clients and the students in my contemplative psychology classes said, "You need to put these ideas into a book!" During my nine years at Gampo Abbey, the project was encouraged and supported by Ani Pema Chödrön, who invited me to teach communication classes there, and by regular pep talks from my friends Ani Palmo, Hollis Scott, Les and Louise Collins-St. Marie, and many others. My deepest thanks to you and to all those who patiently transcribed my talks both at the abbey and in Juneau.

Thank you to Richard Reoch, Chuck and Mary Whetsell, Helen Tworkin, Sister Danielle, Karl Brunholtzl, and Tenzin Yongdu for taking the time to read chapters during the early, awkward stages of the manuscript. And special thanks to Emily Sell, Patricia Tate, and Greg Heffron for their invaluable professional help and feedback in editing the preliminary drafts, and additionally to Greg for his contributions and support for Green Light Conversations, our mindful communication workshops in Vancouver. Thanks also to Josie Geller, Lisa Steckler, Paul Belserene, and Daniel Vokey for reading and giving me feedback on the manuscript. Since this project has been carried forward over so many years, I'm sure there are several people whom I've forgotten to mention, so please forgive me and know that your kindness is appreciated. Finally, I can't find the words to express how grateful I am for the tireless, ongoing support, patience, and enthusiastic encouragement given to this project over the years by my family, especially my son, Sheehan Gillis; my sister, Mary Gillis Chiasson; my father, Dr. Jack Gillis; my best friend and dharma sister, Noreen Morris; and above all my wonderful husband, Jerry. Your dedication to this vision and confidence in my work has given me courage, pushed me beyond my comfort zone, and brought this book into a reality. Above all, I'm grateful to my teachers, especially Chögyam Trungpa Rinpoche and Sakyong Mipham Rinpoche, whose vision, wisdom, and confidence have guided my work for decades by illuminating the fundamental goodness of our life, of our relationships, and of human society.

Introduction

I wanted to write this book to share the idea that we can value and learn from all the conversations in our lives, whether they are pleasant, irritating, or seemingly unimportant. This is what practicing mindful communication means to me. Training in this way leads to the realization that human relationships are naturally "we-first." It shows us that all the gestures or words we exchange with each other originate from a deep human longing for connection, for acknowledgment and appreciation. We want to be seen, heard, and known for who we are, to have our accomplishments celebrated and our suffering comforted. And, when we look more closely, we find that we have an equal need to see, hear, and know others for who they are, to celebrate their joy and empathize with their pain. This mutual need is a fundamental "win-win" that underlies our communication and our relationships, analogous to discovering the root system that connects all the trees that appear to be standing alone in a forest. When we create the time and space to feel our inner longing for authenticity, we realize it is inseparable from our capacity to listen and be touched by others. This we-first view about our relationships is one of the central ideas related to the practice of mindful communication in this book.

We-first vision means that we live and communicate in a dynamic, energetic mixing zone that is essentially interdependent. Like the beauty and power of the natural world around us, this mixing zone of human communication is something we take for granted. But when mindlessness takes over, we try to suppress and overrule this way of knowing, planting "me-first" stakes in the ground and defending our territory. The challenge of mindful communication practice is to see these confused communication habits with sympathy and insight. We notice how they breed a culture of fear and mistrust that keeps our attention focused away from our authentic human nature. We spin story lines based on emotional hunger and aggression. The dividing lines between us become more complicated and we forget that our original need was simply to connect. When the culture of fear spins out of control and things start falling apart, we have an opportunity to get back to basics and ask, "What do I really want?" We need to recover a feeling of being genuinely connected to others, as many of us do when we learn we are going to die soon. The way to do this is by practicing mindfulness, returning the fullness of our attention to what is happening in the present moment.

Communication is the essence of our relationships, so this book is as much about exploring the nature of relationship as it is about conversations. Using mindfulness, we can develop and expand a we-first approach to all our relationships, beginning with ourselves, then extending to the people we know, and finally into the vision of a society that is inspired by these principles. Very simply, in this context *we-first* means that under all circumstances, including conflict, we try to remain open and maintain respect for the person we are communicating with. It is important to remember that *we-first* isn't about ignoring or abandoning our personal interests. Openness is how we stay connected with ourselves just as much as how we connect with others. The way to cultivate this openness is by practicing mindful communication.

The starting point of this book was in the early 1990s at the request of my clients and the students in my classes on contemplative psychology. I taught them models, such as the cycle of heartless-mind and mindless-heart, that arose from my work in the field of domestic violence. It was a crude effort to capture a teaching that my teacher Chögyam Trungpa Rinpoche had previously given about how love can turn into hatred when we freeze the open space between us. Later, I added the metaphor of the traffic lights as a simple way to explore more deeply the three states of mind that occur when we are open, closed, and in-between. Because my clients and students found this helpful, I was encouraged to keep working on this model.

It isn't easy to find the right language to describe in practical detail these experiences, which are profound but also familiar to most people. So I've chosen to use fresh models, metaphors, and symbols that illuminate the journey of self-discovery that unfolds when we bring mindfulness to our patterns of communication. A glossary at the back of the book will help clarify the meanings of these terms and ideas.

In this book we will be zeroing in on some of the most familiar obstacles that arise from our lifelong habit of "me-first" communication, the defensive barrier that originates from a deep-seated fear that we are isolated individuals and that there is something fundamentally inadequate, or wrong, with who we are. Think of it as the lonely-tree-in-the-forest syndrome. This is the habit of feeling isolated, shutting communication down, and forgetting about the root system of open communication. Instead we follow chain reactions that are triggered by fear. Me-first thinking is supported by a culture of mistrust, the message that it's not safe to be vulnerable. We unintentionally communicate these fears to each other in our conversations by not paying attention to the impact that our words and gestures have on each other. This is what mindless communication leads to. By applying mindfulness, we can reverse this process by creating emotionally safe environments for ourselves and for others. I call these welcoming environments "green zones," and I envision them as stem cells that can grow a culture of kindness in our lives and in the world. A therapist's office is usually associated with this kind of green zone. But we can learn to build them for ourselves. Green zones create a safety net for our whole society, like neighbors who chat on the front porch during a hot summer evening. They provide resilience for individuals and communities during difficult times.

We-first societies are not distant fantasies. They exist here and now if we look for them. For some readers it is easy to envision mutual respect within a one-to-one relationship, or even within a family, but the notion of a we-first society might seem unrealistic. Isn't all human society flawed by greed, corruption, and aggression? Another goal for this book is to demonstrate that the we-first vision is completely practical and has already been accomplished by countless people over many generations. I am indebted to my teacher, Sakyong Mipham Rinpoche of the Shambhala lineage, for his tireless efforts to nurture the view that human society is basically good. In my own life, I've lived and worked in several communities that were intentionally we-first, ranging from a convent school to a feminist shelter for battered women, from an experimental treatment program in a maximum-security prison to a Buddhist monastery. Firsthand experience of living or working in these societies, along with my clinical experience as a marital and family therapist, has given me a down-to-earth, practical understanding of the challenges that we face when we make the intention to be more mindful and open in our communication. Challenging, yes, but definitely possible.

The starting point for creating a "green zone" in our lives is to set aside the time and space for practicing sitting meditation, self-reflection, and other contemplative activities. This is the space in which we can learn to feel the natural tenderness of our hearts, to hear ourselves think, to open up and experience the beauty and chaos of the world around us. Mindful communication includes learning how to open up all our senses and really listen to ourselves, each other, and our world.

In practicing mindful communication, we are shedding familiar habits and relationship styles for new ones. We need support in this transition because it affects our very identity. Who we think we are is influenced by our everyday relationships and conversations. At the same time, our communication patterns contribute to creating our social environment. An angry person lives in an angry world and a generous person lives in a generous world. Understanding this, we-first communities over the centuries have relied on precepts and guidelines to help us create the kind of mindful society we want to live in. In that spirit, this book is a training guide that offers practical tips on how to implement the view of we-first into our lives.

Throughout the book, examples and anecdotes from my life and work illustrate the key points. While the names of some of my friends, family members, and teachers are unchanged, all references to clients, coworkers, and workshop participants in the book are composites.

I hope that this book will encourage some readers to bring trusted friends together to form a green zone, adapting the journal exercises into dialogues. Other readers may prefer to work alone or to skip the exercises altogether. I offer this book as a starting point, not as the final word, in the exploration of what mindful communication can bring to our lives. May we all benefit by creating a kind, gentle, and resilient society, one conversation at a time.

I

Stop, Go, and Wait

Conquer the angry man by love.
Conquer the ill-natured man by goodness.
Conquer the miser with generosity.
Conquer the liar with truth.

—THE DHAMMAPADA

RECENTLY A FRIEND sent me an e-mail with some photos attached. "You'll love these," she wrote. When I opened the photos, I chuckled with delight and shot back to her, "Yes, I love these pictures—so much so that I've already written a book about them!"

The photos circulating around the Internet were of a polar bear and a dog playing together. I first saw them in a *National Geographic* magazine many years ago and was captivated by the story. A dog named Churchill was tied up to a stake in the ice. His owner spotted a starving bear, just out of hibernation, through the window of his cabin. He watched in horror as the bear approached his dog. Feeling powerless to protect his pet from certain death, he grabbed his camera and snapped pictures of the scene unfolding before his eyes. But to his amazement, what he ended up witnessing was how Churchill saved his own life.

As the bear lumbered toward him, Churchill crouched down and wagged his tail. In spite of his ravenous hunger, the bear responded to the signal and switched from predator to playmate. One of the photos shows Churchill and the bear embraced in an affectionate hug as they tumbled and rolled around on the ice. Then the huge polar bear turned and ambled away. Over the next few days, the bear returned to the site several times to play with his new friend.

The *National Geographic* photo essay came into my life at the right moment. I had been preparing to teach a series of workshops on mindful communication, where students would learn practical skills in bringing awareness, insight, compassion, and choice to their communications. In preparation, I was paying close attention to my own interactions, especially with the difficult people in my life.

When I first saw the *National Geographic* photos, I was observing the defensive strategies I used with the hungry bears in my life. Would Robert, the bully coworker coming down the hallway, turn into a teddy bear if I adjusted the signals I was sending? Not likely. But I decided to give tail wagging a try anyway.

In some ways, Robert fit the image of a starving polar bear as he stalked the office, commanding attention and emotionally devouring the rest of us with his crude jokes and predictable opinions. Normally, when he walked into the room, I cringed and put on my mask, which only locked the two of us into another episode in our predator-prey relationship. But it occurred to me that I could arouse a feeling of friendliness rather than cower. Over the following days and weeks, I discovered that I could interrupt my defensive reactions to Robert by bringing up the mental image of Churchill and the polar bear. This interruption in my defensiveness allowed me to relax. In one such moment, I flashed back to my little brother at age four dressed up as a cowboy wearing a sheriff's badge. A wave of sisterly affection came over me, and with it, a new image of Robert. I saw him as a lonely, confused man who was always hungry

because he had no idea how to nourish himself through friendship. Imagining his isolation made me feel sad. Letting my
guard down even for a moment or two allowed me to notice
the vulnerable messages Robert was *really* communicating behind his bravado. I still did not agree with his bullying tactics,
but he became a real human being to me—wounded and
frightened, just like the rest of us.

As Robert came more into focus for me, positive details
about him started to emerge. I appreciated that he was always
on time for work even though his eyes looked tired and swollen, as if he'd been up too late the night before. I noticed that
he had good taste in clothes and that his shirts were always
clean and ironed. Gradually, I formed a more respectful image
of Robert, and my fear of him lessened significantly. I felt my
resistance to him dissolve, and felt some compassion grow. Not
only did I feel better about Robert, I felt better about myself.
Over time I noticed that Robert seemed to pause by the door
of my office more often than he used to, even though he had
nothing in particular to say. I had the impression that he was,
without knowing why, drawn toward the small amount of
warmth I was generating—like a cat to a sunny window ledge.

By merely paying attention to my interactions with Robert,
I had learned two lessons. First, I realized how I distort my
view of other people when I'm reacting defensively. I also saw
that when I can open up and see another person in a fresh way,
my own self-image transforms. On the surface, these two insights might not seem to be that big a deal. Not as exciting as a
dog and a hungry bear rolling around in play. But learning how
to switch out of defensiveness into a more humorous, receptive
state of mind *is* a big deal—it is the key to happy, harmonious
relationships and communities.

I once heard the saying that love and fear can't inhabit the
same room at the same time. The truth of this saying has held up
over the years in practicing mindful communication. It's easy to
feel loving and kind when we're open. I often remind my clients

that good intentions, like well-written wedding vows, are meaningless when we're in love. They only have power when fear enters the room. The hard work of practicing mindful communication is that it brings us face-to-face with our anxieties about relationships. These anxieties are rooted in much deeper, core fears about ourselves, about our value as human beings. The good news is that if we are willing to stay present and relate to these core fears, we discover that the power of love is much greater than the power of fear. Gaining confidence in this discovery, we find that any relationship can be transformed into a path of self-discovery. Simply being mindful of our open and closed patterns of conversation will increase our awareness and insight. We begin to notice the effect our communication style has on other people. We start to see that a fear-based attitude toward a person can blind us to who he or she really is.

THE THREE LIGHTS

In my mindful-communication workshops, the metaphor we use to notice whether communication is closed, open, or somewhere in-between, is the changing traffic light. When the channel of communication closes down, we imagine the light has turned red. When communications feels open again, we say the light has turned green. When communication feels in-between, or on the verge of closing down, we say the light has turned yellow. Participants find that the changing-traffic-light imagery helps them identify their various styles of communication, and to recognize the consequences of each.

We use the green and red lights to highlight open and closed patterns because this isn't something we normally track. Once those are clear, we zero in on the in-between stage of the yellow light. Following is a brief overview of what the lights mean.

The red light indicates that communication has shut down. If we imagine a conversation to be like a two-way flow of traffic, with a balance of information coming from both directions, the red light signals that traffic has stopped. At least one person is not listening. This shutdown can be brief or prolonged. For example, when we feel misunderstood and say, "Could we stop for a moment to make sure we're on the same track?" we may be responding to a brief flash of the red light. A prolonged example can occur when we're in a long-term relationship with someone who is highly defended and opinionated, unable to accept who we are or what we have to say. So the red light can also be used to mark those times when we're open, but the person we're trying to communicate with remains closed, sending a "No Trespassing" message. We also use the red-light signal to understand how we ourselves shut down. When our defensive barriers go up, we block the flow of information from our environment and replace it with mental story lines, projections, fears, and reactions. In all cases, the value of the red light is to serve as a reminder to stop when communication has shut down.

The green light symbolizes openness, when the two-way traffic is flowing in a conversation. It is genuine dialogue, when we go beyond our familiar ideas into uncharted new territory. It is also genuine friendship, when we accept, appreciate, and love others for who they are. On our personal journey, the green light marks brief moments of openness that we can remember and use as guidelines for communication. When we're open, we can listen—to ourselves, to the environment around us, and to other people. Openness shows us three natural gifts that all human beings are born with:

- Awake body, the ability to pay attention
- Tender heart, the ability to empathize with others
- Open mind, the ability to be honest, curious, and insightful.

These three green-light faculties are the basis for mindfulness practice, as we will see in the next chapter.

The yellow light describes the period in between the green

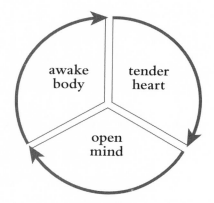

Fig. 1. Natural Communication System

and red light, the gap of groundlessness that occurs just before communication shuts down. We've been caught off guard and we feel embarrassed, irritated, or disappointed by an unexpected event. Below the surface of these reactions, deeper fears and self-doubts are exposed. If we can meet these fears with gentle insight, using mindfulness practice, we can intercept our red-light triggers.

Working with the yellow light is an advanced skill in the practice of mindful communication. Normally we begin by simply noticing the red and green lights—how we open up when we feel emotionally safe, and how we shut down when we feel afraid. Paying attention to these patterns without judging them increases our self-awareness and gives us greater control of our conversations. After we've spent some time observing our patterns of opening up and closing down, we can zero in on this most important area, the stage in between. Mindfulness teaches us how to hold steady when we feel hurt or disappointed. It gives us the power to refrain from making matters worse during those episodes when negative reactions rise up because things aren't going as we planned. Let's go back to my relationship with Robert to learn more.

The Red Light: Defensive Reactions

During an important business meeting, or in the middle of a painful argument with our partner, mindful-communication training can help us recognize when the channel of communication has shut down. With that awareness we remain silent instead of blurting out something we'll later regret. When I let Robert intimidate me, my red light came on. I became defensive and closed down. When we react to fear by shutting down the channel of communication, we've put up a defensive barrier that divides us from the world. In our mind, we justify our defensiveness by holding on to unexamined opinions. We tell ourselves that relationships are not that important. We undervalue other people and put our self-interest first. In short, our values shift to "me-first." Closed communication patterns are controlling and mistrustful. We see others as frozen objects that have importance only if they meet our needs.

The problem with closed communication is that it increases our distress rather than protecting us. Regardless of how self-assured we may feel or appear on the surface, the sense of isolation that our defensive barrier triggers is subconsciously terrifying. If we are indeed isolated individuals, how do we meet our own needs? How do we get our supplies? How do we ward off enemies? Suppressing these inner fears makes us even more rigid and out of touch with the flow of energy in our body, mind, and heart. We tighten our muscles and thoughts; we harden our hearts.

Feeling isolated makes us emotionally hungry, so we look to other people to rescue or entertain us. We manipulate them to get what we need. Because our strategies can't possibly succeed, we become disappointed with people. We suffer, and we cause others to suffer.

Let's make sure we're clear about the difference between healthy self-protection and the fear-based barriers we're talking about. When the light is red, we confuse the two. Genuine self-protection can only be found through openness. When we shift to "me-first," thinking, it's in our self-interest to ignore the impact our words have on others, and we fail to notice that things only get worse and that the protection we're seeking gets farther out of reach.

We're born with sensitive receptors in our body, heart, and mind that keep us tuned into the flow of energy and life going on around us and within us. Each of us already has this natural communication system that feeds us information all the time. So when we close down and become defensive—for a few minutes, a few days, months, or even a lifetime—we're cutting ourselves off, not only from others but also from our natural ability to communicate. Mindful communication trains us to become aware of when we've stopped using our innate communication wisdom, a state symbolized by the red light.

The Green Light: Openness

When I was able to open up and reconnect with my resources, and to reconnect to Robert as a playmate, my green light came on. Paying attention to our communication patterns helps us realize the value of openness. Communicating mindfully brings a greater sense of warmth and honesty to our relationships. Genuine friendship depends on self-acceptance, which is made possible with mindfulness practice.

The green light symbolizes nowness. Mindfulness allows us to notice this. It is the mind's ability to remember what we're doing, to wake up again when our attention wanders too far away from the present moment. Without mindfulness, we'd be unable to drive a car or read a printed page. But like the muscles of our body, the mental power of mindfulness becomes stronger with training and weaker with neglect.

Mindfulness can transform relationships. We nurture relationships by paying attention and we protect them by being mindful of what we say when negativity arises. Like Churchill the dog, staying connected to others, even to our enemies, is a more successful strategy than hiding behind an imaginary barrier and going it alone.

When we are with a good friend, we don't regard our individual needs to be in opposition to the needs of that person. We experience a "we-first" state of mind because we appreciate that our individual survival depends on the well-being of our relationships. We express this sense of connectedness to others in open communication patterns. Open communication tunes us in to whatever is going on in the present moment, whether it is comfortable or not. Openness is heartfelt, willing to share the joy and pain of others. Because we're not blocked by our own opinions, our conversations with others explore new worlds of experience. We learn, change, and expand.

The Yellow Light: The Crisis of Uncertainty

"I don't understand the yellow light," said my friend Kerry's four-year-old daughter one day from the backseat of the car. "I know red means stop and green means go. But when the light is yellow, some people speed up and others slow down."

In mindful-communication training, the symbolic yellow light is a reminder to slow down and take a closer look at what happens when something unexpected occurs, when we feel uncertain. What we're more accustomed to doing is to race right through a yellow in-between state, and then smack right into a red closed state.

When my defensive reactions to Robert became so painful that I began to be curious about them, my yellow light came on. In practicing mindful communication, eventually we ask ourselves, "What exactly causes me to switch from open to closed and then open again?" We begin to discover the state of mind that exists in between open and closed—symbolized by the yellow light. In-between is a place we normally don't want to enter. We find ourselves there when the ground falls out from beneath our feet, when we feel surprised, embarrassed, disappointed—on the verge of shutting down. At this moment, we might feel a sudden loss of trust, an unexpected flash of self-consciousness. Learning to hold steady and be curious at this point is essential to the practice of mindful communication. Buddhist teacher Pema Chödrön, who has been an invaluable mentor for me in this work, uses the word *shenpa* to describe the undercurrent of energy that we feel in this yellow zone. She gives us the instruction to "hold our seat."

If our barriers truly had value, there would be no point to this practice. But our defensive barriers weaken us, like someone who is so afraid of germs that they wear a surgical mask and gloves all the time. Practicing mindfulness is a more effective way to stay healthy. It strengthens our emotional immune system, as it were, so that we are less affected by the small, everyday problems in our relationships.

The in-between state of mind is a critical time for bringing peace into our homes and workplaces. For instance, Jason and Debra wanted to practice mindful communication because they were stuck in negative reactions to each other. They had met three years earlier during a fund-raising drive for a public radio station. Debra was immediately attracted to the small man with a shy smile who was carrying a huge African drum through the crowd. By the end of the evening, after hearing him perform, Debra was in love. When she saw him again the next day, Debra asked Jason if he wanted to go on a daylong kayaking trip with her. He hesitated for a moment as if he were on the edge of a high diving board. Debra had all the qualities he loved in a woman. She was smart, independent, and sexy. He knew this relationship had the potential to be deep, but would it be safe? He took a leap, said yes, and they'd been together ever since.

Three years later, they hit a rough spot. They felt constantly irritated by each other. The very qualities that had initially attracted them had turned toxic. Debra's independence made her seem aloof and unpredictable. Jason's creativity and playfulness made him seem superficial and immature. But they didn't want to abandon their relationship, at least not yet. At the end of our consultation they were surprised by the homework assignment: perform three random acts of kindness for each other every day for the next week. There would be time later to build a better communication bridge, but first Jason and Debra needed to restore an atmosphere of appreciation and gratitude in their relationship.

Small acts of kindness that are either shared or withheld when the yellow light is flashing can make or break a relationship. Once we're in the red zone, it's too late to engage in acts of kindness—we're too mistrustful. I've seen this over and over again. When I work with couples, they typically reach a critical point when they could save their relationship by switching from me-first to we-first thinking. The switch happens if they think about their children, pets, or anything that brings a larger picture to mind. Even a temporary mood of gratitude and shared interest can provide a safety net when things fall apart.

Rather than leaving it up to chance, Debra and Jason made wish lists of small gifts of kindness that made them feel grateful, and attached them to the fridge with a magnet. The agreement was that if the other person offered one of these gifts, the other would say thank-you. The lists included some of the everyday tasks they had taken for granted:

- I appreciate it when you call from work during the day just to say hi.
- I appreciate it when you make dinner or pack my lunch for me.
- I appreciate it when you give me half an hour of quiet time alone.
- I appreciate it when you come with me to a film that I want to see, even if you think you won't like it.

- I appreciate it when you do my laundry for me.
- I appreciate the way you relate to my family, remembering their birthdays for me.

Feeling gratitude for everyday kindnesses made Debra and Jason more interested in moving farther into dialogue with each other. They realized the value of keeping a we-first approach of mutual respect when they went on to talk about their differences. In contrast, they saw how their me-first reactions triggered greater mistrust. Debra put it this way:

> This exercise reminded me of my grandmother's expression, "You can get more with honey than with vinegar." No matter how angry I am about Jason's behavior, I don't want to make things worse with my reactions. I know if I start criticizing him, it will backfire and hurt our relationship even more. So now I start off by thanking him for something positive he's done, and this seems to change the whole tone of what I'm about to say next, not only for him but for me too.

Kindness, gentleness, and gratitude make our yellow-light reactions workable. A we-first approach allows us to be more sensitive to our own anxieties and more patient with others. For instance, I became more sympathetic to Robert after examining my own awkward, self-defeating attempts to guard myself from imaginary threats.

There are also miracle moments when we can open up and wag our tails to play. We break the spell of focusing only on our personal agendas and awaken to genuine relationship. Such abrupt shifts seem to come out of nowhere in the middle of our most ego-crunching experiences—such as admitting that we've made a mistake.

The yellow-light zone is a moment of choice. When I'm in that zone, I can hear my mind debating which direction to go:

do I go back and apologize or continue to hold a grudge? Depending on how much friendliness I bring, I could tip in either direction. The happiness of my marriage hangs on this balance.

When I think back to the ongoing communication process I have with my husband, I realize that our twenty-three-year marriage has been a series of turning points. At these turning points the path of our relationship could have led toward heaven or hell. Our happiness is the result of thousands of small flashes of the yellow light, where we were able to transform disappointments and arguments into opportunities for unmasking, intimacy, and joy.

USING THE THREE LIGHTS AS GUIDELINES

Mindful-communication training isn't directed at intimate relationships alone. It is a personal journey that uses the sensitive emotional ups and downs of everyday conversations as a path of self-discovery. The awakeness of our natural communication system is a thread that runs through every moment of our lives. Practicing mindfulness helps us notice this truth. We can observe ourselves opening and closing in small ways throughout the day. A stranger emerges from a crowded sidewalk and asks us for directions. We sit down with a coworker over coffee to discuss a work project. We manage to pull our child away from the computer long enough to ask how school went today, hoping for more than a one-word reply. The conversation that takes place during a job interview can change the direction of our lives; the words we exchange with the cashier at our local coffee shop might seem less important—but every interaction creates an emotional imprint on us. Even in a crowd of strangers, we human beings are always influencing one another, one way or another. Some people can uplift our spirits without saying a word, such as the janitor humming a tune while he mops the floor in a large office building. Others can deflate our mood with one cynical remark.

The Intention to Be We-First

Most of the people who attend mindful-communication retreats and workshops are motivated by the wish to genuinely
help others. There is a palpable sadness in the room when we
describe how powerless we feel on the other side of the closed-
communication door when someone we love has cut us off.
Feeling the depths of this sadness is a useful starting point for
our work together. Realizing that we feel powerless to help
others is like hitting bottom. We're ready to let go of the strategies we've been using to try to control each other and try something new.

The dysfunctional me-first approach is like a rogue state
that militarizes its borders while the citizens inside are starving.
We defend ourselves as if we were isolated individuals, cut off
from the world around us. Intellectually we might disagree
with this view, but emotionally this is what happens when our
barriers go up. When I wall myself off, I have only three preoccupations: to get my needs met, to push away or punish anyone
who threatens me, and to ignore feedback. According to the
psychology of mindfulness, these three impulses—craving, aggression, and ignorance—are responsible for creating the illusion of the false self. This false self makes us feel like we're a big,
solid rock in the middle of a river, resisting the flow. The great
sadness that motivates us to practice mindful communication
comes from seeing how much suffering these familiar me-first
communication patterns cause.

Sadness and the longing to help others are like jet fuel for
practicing mindful communication. The slogan "Go with the
green light" refers to a certain kind of power we've been over-
looking until now. Under all circumstances, even with an enemy
approaching, we can draw from the power of relationship instead of reacting defensively. This is the power of we-first.

We-first is shorthand for the paradigm shift that happens
when we open up. It means that we can identify with relation-

ship itself rather than with our individualism. Another word for this is *selflessness*. Many of us are skeptical about the word *self-lessness* because we associate it with being a martyr or a goody-goody. But openness shows us a positive kind of selflessness, a win-win view in which the way to help ourselves is by helping others. My teacher Chögyam Trungpa Rinpoche describes genuine selflessness as the final stage in a long journey of opening communication:

> It takes a long time to take our fences down. The first step is to learn to love ourselves, make friends with ourselves, not torture ourselves anymore. And the second step is to communicate to people, to establish a relationship and gradually help them. It takes a long time and a long process of disciplined patience. If we learn to not make a nuisance of ourselves and then to open ourselves to other people, then we are ready for the third stage—selfless help.[1]

One important lesson I've learned from practicing these teachings is that they are deceptively easy to talk about and extraordinarily challenging to put into action.

Narrow Passages

Years ago, my twelve-year-old son and I packed up the car in Boulder, Colorado, and headed for Alaska. There are many coastal villages and towns in Alaska that you cannot reach by road, including the capital city of Juneau, so the ferry system is called the Alaska Marine Highway. When we reached Bellingham, Washington, we were told it would take two days and three nights for the boat to wind its way up the coast to Juneau, taking the Inside Passage route, which cannot be navigated by larger vessels. On the third night I set my alarm clock for three A.M. so that we'd be sure not to miss the Wrangell Narrows, a treacherous twenty-two mile channel through the Alexander Archipelago.

"Wake up, Sheehan, I have a surprise for you," I said with a nudge. He mumbled something, rolled over, and then, on second thought, roused himself for the adventure. We huddled in a blanket on the deck in the chilly, dark mist and watched the silhouette of the shoreline gradually emerge as the ship approached the dangerous corridor between the islands. It was an eerie, dreamlike atmosphere that felt like Dante's journey into Hades. The ship's engine had slowed, and it felt like we were drifting. Then, out of the blackness, lights appeared, blinking green and then red.

"Wow, that is so cool!" my son exclaimed for both of us.

Over the next few hours, the ship was carefully guided through the narrows by about sixty navigational lights posted on buoys. I told Sheehan that these lights meant the difference between life and death for thousands of fishing boats and small ships. As we slipped along through the dark sea, following the guidance of the lights, I felt a surge of gratitude for my teachers.

For decades I'd been fortunate to receive a steady stream of profound and paradoxical teachings on mindfulness from some of the greatest meditation masters in the world. Like the explorers and navigators who created a safe passage through these hazardous waters, my teachers have charted the journey that has shown me what to cultivate and what to refrain from in my relationships. They are like blinking green and red lights in the darkness for travelers like me.

The qualities of openness are like flashes of light in a dark night. These qualities are radically different from what's valued by our dominant society: mindlessness and speed. It's hard to slow down enough to discover the open quality of communication. Instead, we're mostly concerned with strategies to get what we need. Our fear-based society is preoccupied by a me-first view, and this is shown by the insatiable hunger of our consumerism, our continuous paranoia over unseen enemies, and the numbing way we're encouraged to lose ourselves in mindless entertainment. These influences are the rocky shoals that make the practice of mindful relationship so perilous.

Fear-based environments make us lose perspective, which is why we need the guidance of enlightened teachers. What we're told is normal may actually be toxic, and this can be very hard to see. It's like the fable about the village well that became poisoned. Everyone who drank the water from this well went crazy, one by one. If you were to go to a village where everyone was crazy, you'd begin to doubt your own sanity too.

Using that analogy, when we wake up to the truth of interdependence, we see the craziness of our strategies to promote ourselves by harming others. Mindless communication means that anything goes when we're protecting or promoting our own interests. However, suppose that in the middle of an argument, we find ourselves about to unleash a secret verbal weapon against someone and instead ask ourselves, "Do I really want to cause permanent harm to this relationship?" At such a moment, it's as if the influence of the poisoned well has worn off—we're having a moment of sanity. Practicing mindful communication is like remembering to drink fresh water from a well that isn't poisoned. It is like having an enlightened teacher whisper in our ear.

New Ideas

To understand the view of we-first, we need to look for different systems of thought and cultures that aren't fear-based. As Albert Einstein famously said, "Problems cannot be solved by the level of awareness that created them." Look around and find those people who are engaged in solutions rather than creating problems. Who are the ones in your life who operate from that level of awareness?

I was introduced to the idea of "we-first" by my father. On my eleventh birthday, a seventy-five-pound golden lab named Smallwood joined our family. That dog made a memorable entrance. From the moment he leaped through the front door, nothing went as planned. He was so strong and cheerful that his wagging tail knocked my toddler sister flat on her back. With Smallwood's arrival, a new chapter opened in my life, for I began going for evening walks with the dog and my dad. After the dishes were done, we'd slip out of the hot, noisy house and into the foggy, twilit streets of our neighborhood. Over the next couple of years, during these walks, my dad introduced me to the great ideas he was reading about.

Dad was enthusiastic about the writings of Erich Fromm, Viktor Frankl, Eric Berne, Rollo May, and others. All of these great thinkers were talking in one way or another about the power of love and openness. Dad described Martin Buber's philosophy, which compared two kinds of communication: genuine dialogue, which he named "I/Thou," which is open, and its opposite, "I/it," which is closed. When we're closed, we turn others into "it," into an object. Similar ideas were expressed by psychologist Carl Rogers, who described healing communication as "unconditional positive regard." Later, physicist David Bohm defined genuine dialogue as "a stream of meaning that flows among, through us and between us."[2]

When I listened to my dad describing all these new ideas, I realized that "openness" is a kind of paradigm shift from another way of being. I understood that there was a human state of mind of unconditional warmth and curiosity that was available when our barriers dissolve. This openness brings a sense of sacredness and respect to our lives. Buber honored this we-first style of relationship by using the word *Thou*.

In contrast to I/Thou communication, Buber says that when we turn away from this openness, we're in the paradigm of I/it. We lose the magic and dehumanize our relationships, turning people into objects to be manipulated in some way. Disconnecting like this, we reduce everything to an object, cutting ourselves off even from our own body, heart, and mind. This me-first system is how we justify activities that destroy the natural world and perpetuate fear-based societies.

The 1960s were an unsettled time of change, a time of conflict, war, and social revolution. New ideas about the power of love and openness were a catalyst for my generation. In the words of Dr. Martin Luther King Jr., "Love is somehow the key that unlocks the door which leads to ultimate reality."[3] During those walks with my dad I felt a new kind of spirituality dawning, a comprehensive view of sacredness that included psychology and relationships. It deepened my understanding of open communication. For me, closing the door on an evening of television and stepping outside with my dad was a rite of passage, a transformational dialogue that continues to this day.

Since then, I've encountered more great teachers who have dedicated their lives to charting the dangerous passage through fear-based systems. They show us that a gentle, enlightened society isn't some future goal. When we open, it manifests on the spot. By example, these teachers show us what selflessness looks like. They point out the natural qualities that are inherent in each of us. They also give paradoxical instructions, showing us that the way to open communication is through compassionately understanding its opposite—how we shut down.

Like navigational lights that shine in the dark, the insights from our teachers provide a sharp contrast to our confusion. They show us how to be compassionate with our sense of failure. Let's face it, if there were a shortcut that bypassed the embarrassment of seeing our own foibles, I'm sure we'd all take it. But such a shortcut would also shortchange us, because our genuine powers of communication can only arise by making a relationship with our habits of mindlessness rather than pretending they aren't there. They cannot be gained any other way. By definition, mindlessness is hard to see. So, even though it's embarrassing, it's good news to discover that it's an open secret. Our external conversations broadcast the confused story lines that go on in our mind.

To bring these conversations into our practice, we use three slogans that summarize the instructions on what to cultivate, what to refrain from, and how to work with the core fears that surface in between:

1. *Go with the green light.* The first instruction describes setting the intention to be more open, which means being less self-absorbed and more available for others. When we're open, we're cultivating friendship with ourselves as the basis for a we-first approach to relationships, respecting our connection to other people regardless of the ups and downs that occur in our communication.

2. *Stop when the light is red.* The second instruction is to refrain from harmful communication patterns. Using mindfulness, we can replace me-first barriers with a more skillful way of protecting ourselves without damaging our relationships. The first step is to learn to recognize closed conversation patterns—the red light—and then to learn to stop and let go instead of pushing forward into the danger zone. Stopping at the red light gives us the space to be curious about what happens when communication shuts down. In this space we can learn to replace defensive habits with a more realistic way of responding when problems arise.

3. *Be careful when the light is yellow.* Refraining from harmful communication makes it possible to explore the vulnerable doubts and fears that lie beneath our red-light habits. The yellow light symbolizes the triggers that normally lead to shutting down. Like ice thawing in the warmth of the sun, these fears melt when we join them with warmth and inquisitiveness. We need to be careful about the voices we listen to during these sensitive transition times so that we can make room for our fears while at the same time not buying into them. To do this, we seek support from people who share a similar we-first intention.

Understanding this process shows us that mindful communication depends on making room to observe our own red-light patterns rather than judging them as bad. At the same time, we gently refrain from acting them out. The threefold instruction of the slogans is how we reclaim the parts of ourselves that we've rejected and gradually extend that friendliness to others. In the process, we restore greater harmony to our families and communities.

JOURNAL EXERCISE

Write your own vision statement for the first slogan, "Go with the green light." Who are the people in your life who have contributed to this vision?

THE FIVE KEYS

The five keys to mindful communication are methods for genuinely helping others by relating to our fears and misunderstandings and working patiently with our communication challenges. They are as follows:

1. *The key to mindful presence: awake body, tender heart, open mind.* Mindlessness keeps us depressed and anxious, too restless to listen, even to ourselves. By making a relationship with this restlessness, we reconnect with our own basic healthiness, sanity, and goodness, which enables us to function as healers.

2. *The key to mindful listening: encouragement.* Discovering how we mindlessly build ourselves up by putting others down, we can learn to cultivate genuine confidence instead of arrogance. Recovering our own self-worth opens the door to seeing value in others. This is the path of the nurturing leader or parent who can see the "heart of gold" in others and envision their potential.

3. *The key to mindful speech: gentleness.* By refraining from the two extremes of exaggerating and silencing, we can use mindfulness to uproot aggressive communication patterns and gently refocus our attention on things as they are.

4. *The key to mindful relationships: unconditional friendliness.* Mindfulness is blocked by the conditions we bring to relationships. When we recognize this red-light pattern, we start to see our hidden agendas and realize how challenging it is to accept others as they are. The path of working with disappointment unmasks our unrealistic expectations and exposes destructive relationship patterns. As we do this, our capacity for unconditional friendliness expands.

5. *The key to mindful action: playfulness.* Communicating mindfully is not like walking down the street to work. It's more like dancing with your lover in the kitchen, but your lover is the present moment. Responding skillfully is the result of being synchronized with our natural communication system of open mind, tender heart, and awake body. We know what to do because each next step in this dance is revealed to us as we go along. We learn how to do this by relating with our control issues. When we're competing with reality, trying to master or conquer it, we're pushing against something that feels separate from ourselves.

In the following chapters, we'll explore these five keys in more detail as we learn how to work with the inspirations and obstacles along the way in the journey of mindful communication.

2

The Key to Mindful Presence
Awake Body, Tender Heart, Open Mind

Meditation takes us just as we are, with our confusion and our sanity. This complete acceptance of ourselves as we are is called *maitri,* a simple, direct relationship with the way we are.

—PEMA CHÖDRÖN

WHEN MARTINA WALKS into a room, everyone notices. Her charisma isn't like the big splash that a politician or movie star cultivates. It's more like a pebble that drops into a pond, with widening circles rippling outward that have a soothing effect on everyone. As her friend, I've seen this happen many times in various situations and have tried to pinpoint exactly what it is that she does to command this kind of power. What I notice is that she seems to carry the posture and mood of meditation with her at all times. The uplifted quality of her body transforms her movements into dance. And there always seems to be space around her, as if she's floating in a different dimension from the rest of us. The beauty of Martina's presence is that this ripple effect seems completely natural to her. She's as friendly and unself-conscious as a child.

Communication experts tell us that most of the information we convey is nonverbal. What Martina communicates is gentle vulnerability, the unconditional friendliness that comes from integrity. Her body, heart, and mind function as an integrated whole rather than being disconnected from one another. This is the first power of mindful communication: mindful presence. It is warm, bright, and all pervading, like sunlight diffused through space.

Martina's presence is accommodating because she's made friends with an inner solitude. Because of her mindfulness practice, she appreciates silence and space. This inner solitude gives her a sense of freedom. You feel that she can deeply listen to herself as well as to others. When she speaks, this spaciousness makes her words more effective. When Martina wants to have a meaningful conversation with someone, she creates a welcoming environment, asking, "Is this a good time for you to talk?" rather than jumping right in. It feels like you're being ushered into an elegant restaurant rather than grabbing a sandwich on the run. She offers a similar quality of attention to herself. Every day she sets aside space and time for her personal meditation practice.

MEDITATION: RECONNECTING WITH BODY, HEART, AND MIND

The starting point for genuinely listening to others is learning to listen to our own body, heart, and mind, the basic intelligence of the present moment. The slogan "Go with the green light" means we gain the power of mindful presence by learning to recognize these experiences and to cultivate them. Mindfulness meditation is an important way to do this.

Meditation trains our minds to pay attention by allowing thoughts to flow naturally rather than being captivated by them. Because our words are an expression of our thoughts, meditation is a powerful aid to relationship. Having a little quiet time when we can relax and accept ourselves as we are helps us be more open to others.

Practicing mindfulness meditation is taking a break from our struggle to survive. Instead of leaning toward our future plans or burdening ourselves with worries from the past, we can simply sit down and relax in the present moment. This is how the power of mindful presence dawns. Mindfulness meditation is more of an un-training than trying to do something new. Meditation tunes us in to the flow of our natural communication system. Let's take a closer look at what this means. This communication system operates at the most fundamental level of our awareness, where we accommodate the first moment of an experience. The three ways we receive this information are as follows:

- Awake Body: coming back to our senses
- Tender Heart: trusting our heart
- Open Mind: being open and flexible

Here's how Lucy, a participant in a mindful-communication retreat, described her experience of these three:

Yesterday I was walking out of a parking lot when a homeless man approached me. Before I could turn my eyes away, I noticed a bloody cut across his forehead. I was outside my comfort zone, but I realized that my sense perceptions were awake.

Lucy's sense perceptions caught her attention and put her in relationship to this homeless man regardless of whether she wanted to or not. She continued:

When I saw the bloody wound on the man's forehead, it wasn't out of cold, scientific curiosity. I felt sorry for him.

Thanks to the natural tenderness of her human heart, Lucy responds to this man's suffering without distinguishing whether he is a stranger or a friend.

> I got curious about this guy. What had happened to him? How did he get this cut on his head? I wondered about his life, his pain, his future. All of this happened in one instant, and then it was over and I continued on my way down the street.

Lucy related with the homeless man even though she didn't want to. Her conscious intention had been to ignore him, to avoid the discomfort of relating to him. She was preparing herself to put up a barrier, but in spite of that urge, something genuine occurred.

Reconnecting to Awake Body through Posture

We cultivate the natural wakefulness of body, heart, and mind with meditation practice. The foundation of mindfulness practice is reinhabiting our body. To do this, we need to restore our natural uprightness. There is a slogan for this instruction: "Strong back, soft front." "Strong back" means that our backbone is uplifted, straight but supple, like a tree planted into the earth. With this strong back holding us up, we can soften and open up our heart area. Remember what it felt like to be a young child sitting on the kitchen floor? That's it.

Place your hands on your thighs in an ordinary way, so that your upper body feels balanced. For some of us, sitting cross-legged on a cushion is the easiest way to meditate. But we could also sit on a chair, with feet planted on the floor like the roots of our tree. Restoring the flow of energy from the top of our head down to the soles of our feet reconnects us with the larger world, the sky overhead, and the earth below.

The upright meditation posture has a calming effect on our

mind. Our natural body-heart-mind is a network of flowing currents of energy that are unblocked when we learn how to relax and sit still with a good posture. There's a certain strength that comes with this dignified posture. Getting ready for a first date or a job interview, we instinctively know what this means.

Relaxation is the key to mindfulness practice, but at the same time we need to arouse our natural wakefulness. So another slogan is "Not too tight, not too loose." Relax your jaw and throat by exhaling through your mouth and silently saying "ahhhh." That is how your throat area can open during meditation. But you can keep your lips closed if you like.

This style of meditation doesn't aim for a trance state, so we keep our eyes open. Placing our gaze downward about three to four feet in front of us, we simply rest our vision there like parking a car. Then we gently bring our attention to the rising and falling of the breath as it moves in and out of our body.

Key points about posture:

- Back is straight but flexible; strong back, soft front.
- Relax throat and jaw by saying "ah".
- Let your breathing be natural.
- Keep your eyes open; relax your gaze at a point about three feet in front of you.
- Put your hands on your thighs.
- Sit cross-legged, or if you are in a chair, plant both feet evenly on the floor.

Reconnecting to Tender Heart with Our Breath

Because mindfulness meditation is training ourselves to stay present, we could use any object as a way to return to nowness. My teachers recommend using our breath. Our breath is a vital link that connects our body, heart, and mind, so it is an excellent method for integrating our natural communication system. If your mind feels wild, you can count your breath, from one to ten and then back to one again. Or, if you feel more relaxed, you can simply identify your attention with the flow of the out-breath, dissolving into the space around you. There is a natural gap at the end of the breath. We use this gap as a way of relaxing—ahhh. Then we follow the in-breath, returning to a sense of embodiment.

If using the breath is too difficult, you could use a more concrete object, such as a rock, and place it in the visual field in front of you. Then rest your attention on it. Whenever your attention wanders, gently bring it back. The point isn't to study the object, but simply to use it as a marker that you come back to, a way of noticing that you're here, in the present moment.

Reconnecting to Open Mind by Letting Go

In this practice, we silently say the word *thinking* whenever we realize that we've become distracted from our object of attention. It is like waking up out of a daydream. The point of open-minded meditation isn't to try to get rid of thoughts. The point is merely to relax, unfreeze the mind, and allow the thoughts to flow instead of getting tangled up in them. This technique teaches us to notice that our stream of thoughts has gaps in it, little flashes of green light that we can use to wake ourselves up. It's a profound insight to notice that our mind has the ability to wake itself up. Mindfulness strengthens this ability by placing a value on that flash of interruption.

Once we notice the gap in our thoughts, we can detach from our thought patterns and return to the breath. Distraction is the mindlessness of being carried away by thoughts and emotions. The hard work of mindfulness meditation is learning how to gently detach from those mental activities and come back to our object of attention. Letting go of whatever we're thinking and returning to the object of attention is training in nowness. We become less fascinated by our own inner world so that we can pay better attention to what's going on in front of us. As our minds become more trained, we can use this skill in conversation by resting our attention on another person's body language and their voice.

Meditation helps us develop a peaceful mind by showing us how to let go of thoughts and all the dramas they trigger. Over time, like expanding the lens on a camera, the view gets more spacious. Instead of focusing on our inner conversations, we start to notice the overall patterns of our thoughts—how they gather together and then scatter like a flock of birds.

Key points about meditation:

- To stabilize attention, use a neutral object of some kind to gently bring awareness back whenever you drift off into thoughts. This could be a rock in front of you or your own breath.
- Whenever your attention strays into thoughts, gently interrupt it by saying "thinking" and return to your object.
- Anything that distracts your attention from the object is considered thinking, even if it is an emotion, a sound, a movement, or a sensation.

Accommodating Pain

Mindlessness and speed keep us depressed and anxious, too restless to listen, even to ourselves. By making a relationship with this restlessness, we reconnect with our own basic health-iness, sanity, and goodness. This is why the power of mindful presence is related to the path of the healer. Psychologist Carl Jung describes the archetype of a Wounded Healer, the person who has personally made the journey through his or her own fears and shadows and has emerged with an understanding of what it means to be whole. Wounded healers relate to other people's pain because they've learned to be compassionate with their own fears and limitations. With the power of silent presence we learn to relate to our confusion and grief and to tolerate not knowing. Once we've opened up this relationship to the wounded parts of ourselves, we find there's no dividing line between our own pain and someone else's.

Elizabeth gave me an example of the power of mindful presence when she described the postpartum depression she suffered three months after the birth of her son:

> I was in such a dark place, and on top of that I was ashamed of being so depressed. It felt like I was in a tug-of-war with everyone around me. On one side were all the people who kept trying to cheer me up by telling me how happy I should be at having such a beautiful, healthy little boy. They made me feel like a complete failure. On the other side were the people who were afraid that I'd commit suicide. All they wanted was to give me enough drugs so that the pain would go away.
>
> I went to a clinic and spoke to a counselor. He just sat there and listened to me as I tried to explain what was happening to me. It slowly dawned on me that something different was going on. He was making room for my pain. At one point he leaned forward and asked what my depression was telling me. It was the first time that someone didn't see my pain as an enemy, but that there might be some sanity buried in it somewhere. He encouraged me to listen to myself the same way he was listening to me. I got the feeling that he trusted me and that I could trust myself. I never met him again and I've always wished I could thank him. That conversation was a turning point for me.

Mindful presence is accommodation, the gentle space of a healing relationship. Christian contemplative Henri Nouwen describes opening to pain without struggling to push it away or cure it:

When we honestly ask ourselves which people in our lives mean the most to us, we often find that it is those who, instead of giving us advice, solutions or cures, have chosen rather to share our pain and touch our wounds with a warm and tender hand. The friend who can be silent with us in a moment of despair or confusion, who can stay with us in an hour of grief and bereavement, who can tolerate not knowing, not curing, not healing, and face with us the reality of our powerlessness, that is a friend who cares.[1]

Meditation and self-reflection allow us to become this kind of friend to ourselves. We simply make room for those parts of our experience that we've rejected. We realize that the temporary insanity of our red-light reactions is caused by not knowing how to relate properly to fear and pain.

The problem with mindlessness is like Elizabeth's experience of the tug-of-war—it keeps triggering us to shut down without our knowing why. We are chronically self-absorbed, in crisis mode, because we don't know how to listen to our own distress signals. Meditation practice reverses this condition, teaching us to relax and realign our body, heart, and mind with the world around us. In this way you could think of it as the ultimate healing journey.

Elizabeth's story reminded me of the horse-whisperer, who sits down in a field and waits for hours until the injured horse finally learns how to trust him. When it comes to working with our bodies, hearts, and minds we need the same approach. With an attitude of sympathy for this exhausted, untrained horse of our psyche, we sit down and meditate. Over time we learn how to trust ourselves. We witness the ongoing conversations in our mind without buying into them.

In our own lives, as humble as it seems, practicing sitting meditation means reclaiming our natural inheritance as a human being on this earth. When anxiety or depression takes hold of us, meditation awakens an unconditional friendliness that eventually conquers the belief that we are cut off, the notion that we don't belong here. At the same time, meditation gently eliminates our self-centered habits so that we can turn our attention outward again. Reconnecting with openness is how we build families and societies that give other people the same rights and values that we give to ourselves. This is why the path of mindfulness meditation is often called the warrior's way.

Suggestions for maintaining a practice:

- Find a place that feels right to you and create an environment that reflects dignity, warmth, and openness.
- Choose a time of day when you feel alert.
- Turn off phones and other distractions.
- Decide on a length of time and stick with it, using a timer or a piece of incense.

POSITIVE INTERRUPTIONS

In the first chapter we saw that the basis for mindful-communication practice is simply paying attention to the way we open and close. We discover that openness isn't something we accomplish by force. It dawns upon us as our attention shifts to the wakefulness of our body, heart, and mind. Building on this insight, with the help of meditation practice, we can move on to a second practice. We can abruptly cut through our distractions with a method I call *positive interruptions*. This is similar to the practice of meditation, allowing little flashes of the green light to bring us back to the present moment.

Practicing positive interruptions is like poking holes of wakefulness into our mindless communication habits. Most people don't like interrupting a train of thought, but in this practice we regard interruption as a good thing. We're interrupting our distracted mind and coming back to being fully alive, in the present moment. Instead of constantly filling every gap in our conversations with meaningless chatter, we learn how to pause and allow ourselves to breathe, to reconnect with ourselves.

When my mother was a child, she was playing with a sharp pencil and accidentally poked a hole in her mother's favorite silk lampshade. She felt terrible about it and wondered how she could fix the situation. Then an idea came to her. She knew that her mother loved polka-dot dresses, so she decided to turn the lampshade into polka dots. So she poked hundreds of holes into the lampshade, thinking of how happy this would make her mother. When her mother came in and gasped, "Oh, my God!" there was one blissful moment of suspense before the little girl realized her mother wasn't delighted by the surprise.

I think about this story with a smile when I visualize the practice of positive interruptions. We're poking holes and letting the light of wakefulness come through. But there is another part of ourselves that gasps with horror at the prospect. Our habit of mindlessness wants to keep the shade intact. We don't want to be interrupted by silence or openness, because we feel we need mindless entertainment as a way of avoiding boredom. What is this restless boredom we're trying to escape? How do we get lost in activities of all kinds: the deadlines of a busy schedule, the incessant background commentaries from radio, TV, or the news, the text messages popping up on our cell phones? Asking these kinds of questions is a bit irritating because the question itself is poking a hole in our mindlessness.

Mindful conversations are punctuated by silence here and there, like turning off a TV show and stepping out to breathe the fresh air. If we're absorbed in our TV show, we don't welcome interruptions. Mindless story lines gain momentum from speed and restlessness. We've spent our entire lives in this mindlessness training. Some of us don't like being interrupted even when our personal TV show makes us unhappy. Our familiar comfort zones are more familiar than comfortable.

Going along with the gaps of positive interruptions is one way to practice going with the green light. Mindfulness practice cultivates this natural wakefulness in four ways:

- Allowing silence by deliberately interrupting our conversations and activities with a mindfulness bell
- Coming back to our senses, being positively interrupted by the basic wakefulness of our body
- Being interrupted by a flash of empathy, the tenderness of our heart
- Letting our opinions be interrupted by a moment of doubt from open mind

Interruptions from Silence

> Before you speak, ask yourself: is it kind, is it necessary, is it true, does it improve on the silence?
>
> —SAI BABA

The Zen master Jakusho Kwong Roshi describes the way his teacher, Suzuki Roshi, communicated. "Often he would talk with his eyes closed, as if he was going somewhere inside to verbalize."

It's a good way to collect yourself when you talk, kind of like a nice deep pause, that you go back to the source and then you verbalize again.[2] This is an example of a communication practice my teacher Chögyam Trungpa Rinpoche described as punctuating our words with space. We practice this first style of positive interruption by intentionally bringing gaps into our conversations, opening the space for genuine listening. When we're speaking, we can go back to the source of our own words, listening to ourselves.

There are three benefits that come from adding more silence to our conversations:

- Silence protects our mindfulness practice, making it easier to pay attention to whatever we're doing in the present moment.
- Silence enables us to deeply listen to our environment. This includes the words as well as the subtle messages from other people.
- Silence tunes us in to our natural communication system, the intuitive way of knowing that flows beyond the level of words.

When we're hiking along a beautiful forest trail with a friend, silence doesn't feel like an interruption. It feels natural to let our conversation fall apart from time to time so that we can share a deeper experience beyond words—the sounds, colors, and smells of the natural world around us. In our speedy modern society, we don't like silence. We're more like someone hiking in the woods while talking nonstop on a cell phone. We seem to have an unspoken agreement to avoid silence and stay distracted. When mindlessness rules, silence feels out of place, like the dead air on the radio or TV. We forget what we are missing.

I remember a time in college when even a short gap of silence felt uncomfortable. But years later I spent nine years at Gampo Abbey, a Buddhist monastery, where much of our time was spent in silence. It wasn't a dead kind of silence. It was more like the listening space you feel on a quiet beach as you look out to sea, when you feel like the unseen energies of the place completely permeate your whole being.

To cultivate silence within our conversations, the spiritual director of the abbey, Pema Chödrön, teaches "the pause practice" by asking someone to ring a bell periodically to interrupt whatever is going on at the moment. At the sound of the bell we drop what we're saying and pause for the length of three cycles of breathing. Then we resume as if nothing unusual had occurred. During the gap we have an opportunity to feel the contrast that openness brings, and sometimes this is a bit like feeling suspended in midair.

The pause practice gives us a quick exit from the momentum of conversations so that we can remember the power of silence to reconnect us with the present moment. One way to adapt this practice is to use the ring of a cell phone or a red traffic light as a reminder to pause for a moment, take a deep breath, let your thoughts and words fall apart, and just listen.

One of the most memorable interruptions for me happened the summer after my son and I stepped off the ferry for a new life in Alaska. I had a new job at a local counseling center and, as a single parent, I needed to find activities that would interest an active twelve-year-old while I was at work. Across from my office building was an intriguing little leather goods shop called Nina's Originals. In the window was a faded photo of a young woman modeling a stylish leather coat and hat amid a display of moccasins and slippers. A little bell tinkled when the door opened into the small one-room space, hazy with cigarette smoke. Unchanged for forty years, the walls were cluttered with framed art of all sizes and tastes. All the surfaces were piled with seal pelts, leather and fabric and in one corner was an antique dresser with a long mirror. In the center, behind a table with a sewing machine, lamp, ashtray, and three or four empty coffee cups sat Aunt Dawn, a shy, gentle woman in her early sixties, who had been keeping the business going after her mother, Nina, died. From morning to night the shop was open, but rarely for business. Instead people would drop by, sit, and chat. They were all locals, old friends and family catching up on the latest gossip. If a tourist happened to pause by the window, the chatter dissolved into silent anticipation.

I wandered into the shop a few days after my job began. I'd enrolled Sheehan in a basketball camp, but he hated it. Chatting with Aunt Dawn, she mentioned that her nephew's daughter, who was the same age, was in town. She was sure they wouldn't mind letting him tag along. I was willing to take a chance. I briefly met Jerry, Dawn's nephew, and found him pleasant enough, "kind of boring but not a child abuser," I thought. Over the next few weeks Sheehan told me about the adventures they were having, hiking up Mount Juneau, checking out the cruise ships, or watching movies on rainy days. On the Fourth of July, Dawn invited us to their annual family picnic, a gathering of relatives and friends with as many dogs as people.

Jerry's daughter had returned home to Oregon, so the three of us, Jerry, Sheehan, and I split off from the group to take a hike through the forest to a remote beach. When we got there, I sat down to read a book, and the two of them wandered off to the water's edge to skip rocks.

I was absorbed in my novel but was interrupted by the sound of laughter. I looked up and around, surprised. This laughter was like music, so free and delightful. Who could it be? Then I looked over and realized it was Jerry. My first impression of this man was wrong. Catching a glimpse of who he really was, hearing his laughter, I felt magnetized to him. And this interruption was the starting point of a twenty-three-year love affair.

When we're driven by speed and mindlessness, we ignore or edit most of what our senses are telling us. We might even overlook the love of our life. But thank goodness our natural communication system of awake body, tender heart, and open mind can interrupt our preoccupations in an abrupt way.

Interruptions from Awake Body: Coming Back to Our Senses

The second practice is to welcome the positive interruptions from our sense perceptions and recognize them as a flash of openness, or green light. The whisper of the broom when we're sweeping the floor or the burning sensation on our tongue from the first sip of hot tea brings us back to our ongoing relationship with reality. They show us that every experience in our life is equally precious and worthwhile.

Our body is awake to everything going on around us. Opening the channel of communication with our own body allows us to appreciate the sights, sounds, smells, tastes, and textures all around us. We can touch our experience directly, gaining confidence that we know what we know. No one has to talk us into believing that the sky is blue or the grass is green. We can taste the subtle flavor of a cantaloupe without ever finding the right words to describe it.

Living in Juneau, because the wildlife was such a powerful presence in our everyday lives, these kinds of interruptions happened all the time. There was no such thing as an ordinary commute to work. Here's an example.

One day Jerry and I were driving home from work along the highway, absorbed in a conversation. Suddenly, something unusual interrupted us. Right in front of us a king-sized salmon appeared out of nowhere, falling out of the clear blue sky.

We were slowing down for a red light when this happened. A moment earlier I'd absentmindedly noticed three eagles soaring and diving in the sky high above. Two of them were trying to grab a salmon that the third one was holding, but in the struggle the fish must have slipped away from all three. Across the highway, a hitchhiker with a broad-brimmed hat had no idea what was going on above him. For one horrible instant it looked like the falling fish would land on his head. When it splat-landed a few feet behind him, those of us who were watching from our cars cheered spontaneously in relief. Then the traffic light changed from red to green and we all continued on our way.

Awake body brings us abrupt moments of openness all the time, though they aren't usually as dramatic as a salmon falling out of the sky. The fellow with the broad-brimmed hat reminded me of what it's like not to notice these experiences. How often do the invisible forces of ignorance dominate my conversations, keeping me oblivious to the magic of the real world going on all around me? A salmon falling out of the sky is quite vivid, but what about more subtle messages from reality, such as a change of expression on my listener's face?

In this present moment, our bodies are tuned in to the environment around us. Try putting this book down for a moment, and simply feel present in your body. Notice how your body communicates with temperature, weight, and all your perceptions. This presence is what interrupts thoughts and brings us back to our senses. At the moment, my feet are cold on the top but warm on the bottom where they meet the wooden floor. I hear the drone of a lawn mower out the window. A warm sensation is gathering in my elbow, turning into an aching warning to find a better support for my arm while I'm writing.

The awakeness of our body is a protector. If we're not paying attention, we might trip or stub our toe. Like a playful child, our body is always poking holes in our mental conversations by showing us something new: *Look, up in the sky—a fish!* A positive interruption is a quick flash of the unedited moment, when we come back to our direct experience. The present moment includes everything we perceive, from the bird chirping on the telephone wire to the rotting banana peel next to the Dumpster in the alley.

Interruptions from Tender Heart: Empathy

The third kind of positive interruption comes from our heart. This is when mindfulness could be recast as *heartfulness*. Empathy is an essential component of genuine communication. Empathy shows us how to listen through our heart. Author Daniel Goleman refers to this power as *emotional intelligence*. When we allow ourselves to be positively interrupted by a message from our heart, we often abruptly change course. The wisdom of our heart spontaneously shows us what to do next. For instance, Maryanne shared the following story during a mindful-communication retreat:

> I was yelling at my eight-year-old son, completely sure I was doing the right thing in telling him how stupid he was for leaving his bike in the park, when suddenly I saw the look on his face. It hit me like an arrow in my heart. I remembered the feeling I had when my mom yelled at me like this. That feeling woke me up and everything seemed to melt.

In mindful-communication training we learn to pay attention to this energetic mixing zone, where the dividing line between "me" and "you" can't be found. This inborn sensitivity is a way of knowing that interrupts me-first preoccupations and restores a sense of connection to others. It is an intuitive way of reading the emotional field around us.

Selflessness interrupts us because we care about other people. Tuning in to our relationships is as important as knowing our individual needs. Empathy can make us uncomfortable at times, but it is also our human capacity to love and to be courageous.

I recently had a conversation with a dying man at a hospice. I asked him about the things in his life he felt proud of. He told me about an incident in his youth when he didn't think twice about pushing another boy out of the path of an oncoming truck. "Everyone was angry with me for doing this. My mother said, 'Don't you realize you could have killed yourself?' But their anger didn't bother me. I knew it was the only thing I could have done." He paused and fell back into the pillow and murmured, "It was good to have an opportunity to save a life."

Our heart's way of listening proves that defensive habits are secondary, like the clothes that we wear on top of our sensitive, naked skin. Mindfulness restores our naked, fresh experience.

Waking up to the present moment is about reconnecting to reality rather than creating another strategy to manage it.

When we start practicing mindful communication, we realize how many of our emotional dramas are self-created. Life is hard enough without having an ongoing soap opera in our minds to deal with. But our thoughts generate all kinds of stories that stir up intense reactions within us. Sometimes these secondary emotions grip us for days on end. Other times they disappear out the window when we catch sight of the rustling autumn leaves. They leave behind a haunting feeling of loneliness that is soft and vulnerable. When this happens, the light has turned green again and we've restored the natural balance of body, heart, and mind.

JOURNAL EXERCISE

List examples of empathy from your own life. Contrast these with defensive, me-first emotional reactions. What are the differences in outcome?

Interruptions from Open Mind: When It's Right to Be Wrong

The fourth kind of positive interruption is letting go into uncertainty—seeing through the cracks in our own fixed ideas. All human beings are gifted with a natural wakefulness that makes us question our own opinions. This positive kind of doubt is like a good friend who asks, Why am I saying this? Geoff described an example:

One of my coworkers is a guy named Roger. Normally we get along pretty well, but last week we got into trouble working on a project together. I realized that we see things from opposite points of view. I'm really good at creative envisioning, but he gets frustrated when things aren't linear. So we reached a breaking point about half-way through the project. He needed to know exactly what the next steps would be and I started to get hot under the collar, feeling like he was boxing me in. I re-acted and said some angry words to him. I walked out and took a break. After I cooled down a bit, I realized that I was wrong. His question about the next steps in our work was a legitimate one, and my reactions had nothing to do with him or with the project. So I went back and apologized. It was interesting to notice how the barrier disappeared.

Changing our mind like this seems like an ordinary turning point that most people can relate to. Yet, it is also remarkable. What exactly is it that makes us stop caring about being right and make room for another person's point of view? What causes our defensiveness to dissolve for no reason at all, the way a dream does upon awakening? I call these kinds of experiences "miracle moments." Surrendering our defensive opinions makes gen-uine relationship possible.

Progressive business leaders have made a similar discovery. In the workplace, they've switched from demanding success into encouraging employees to regard failure and mistakes as valuable lessons. The result is a sharp improvement in creativity and morale. As one CEO put it, "Failure is the only way we learn anything. We need a culture in the workplace that en-courages these creative conversations, sharing what hasn't worked and figuring out solutions together."

Thanks to the interruption of intelligent doubt, we can change our mind, learn new things, and admit we're wrong. The gift of open mind makes us curious enough to be willing to see something new, even if it challenges our own fixed ideas. We call the interruption of open mind "*positive* doubt" because there is also another kind of doubt that is not helpful. This negative self-doubt is what triggers our red-light reactions. It is a lack of confidence in our own heart, mind, and body. Negative self-doubt is what surfaces during periods of uncertainty when the yellow light is flashing.

The Big Mind of Wakefulness

Zen master Suzuki Roshi refers to openness as "big mind." Positive interruptions are like gaps in the clouds—or holes in the lampshade—that let the natural light of big mind penetrate our narrow-minded preoccupations. Big mind is there before our barriers go up dividing the world into "for or against me." It communicates to us through the awakeness of our sense perceptions, the sensitivity of our heart, and the curiosity of our natural intelligence.

When the salmon fell out of the sky, the importance of my future planning disappeared into this big mind. My attention expanded into this space as if it were home, like those eagles soaring through the sky. I felt a sense of relief, like being unburdened by a glance out of the window during a hectic afternoon. This dimension of mind felt spacious and warm. This opening happened without any effort on my part. Big mind was spontaneously there when my ordinary distractions were interrupted.

During a discussion on this topic, a friend commented, "Letting go into big mind made me realize that who I am is a verb, not a noun. My mind is always flowing, forming new ideas and reconnecting with others, testing things out, and dissolving all the time." The natural communication system of body, heart, and mind is like a frequency that we tune in to when we let our fences down. This big mind is we-first. It shows us that our identity isn't solid, but always being cocreated by our relationships and the ongoing flow of communication.

The practice of positive interruptions wakes us up to the present moment by reintegrating the flow of communication from our body, heart, and mind. This is how we gain confidence in letting go of our defensive barriers and masks.

Here's a quick review of the four kinds of positive interruptions:

1. Pausing: allowing silence to be part of our communication
2. Awake body: coming back to our senses by allowing our perceptions to wake us up
3. Tender heart: allowing empathy to wake us up
4. Open mind: changing our mind by questioning the validity of our opinions and emotional reactions

Openness of body, heart, and mind enables us to fall in love, to feel empathy and courage. It is the genuine friendliness that enables us to let go of our opinions and discover how big our minds really are. Big mind is a fluid awareness, a state of knowing. The world around us has the same flowing quality. Being connected to this fluid awareness gives us the power to trust our instincts, the way Churchill the dog trusted his instincts to wag his tail.

ALARM CLOCK EXERCISE

Using a journal or in dialogue with a friend, talk about your own examples of "magic moments," of shifting abruptly from a closed to an open mind.
Examples:

- Being interrupted by the environment or a sense perception
- Being awakened by a flash of empathy when you are angry
- Discovering you were wrong and letting go of your position in the middle of a conflict

Mindful Communication: Reconnecting with Wakefulness

Betsy is the girl in the back row of her high school group photo, hidden except for her glasses appearing over someone else's head. It doesn't bother her at all that she's never noticed. She's good at ignoring things. You can learn a lot from Betsy's body language—chronically slumped, her dirty running shoes unlaced. Betsy is gifted with a natural ability to relax and open up, but those qualities are blocked by fear. Like flowing river water under ice, Betsy's pain was a deep sadness in response to the traumas related to her parents' alcoholism that devastated her childhood home. Sadness was a healthy response to a traumatic situation, but it paralyzed her because her environment didn't offer compassionate support. So she withdraws from real or anticipated pain by spacing out, by fixating on fantasies, movies, or trancelike states of mind. Mentally, she has learned to tune out. Physically, she drags herself around as if she were exhausted. When depression takes hold, she gets trapped in stories about failure and hopelessness.

Betsy feels like there is an invisible wall that keeps her cut off from life, unable to fully participate. She feels unwelcome, especially when depression makes it impossible to socialize. As much as she claims to love her sister, she never calls her. They've given up on keeping in touch. Betsy is always struggling to distract herself. She has a hard time rekindling interest in anything at all. Long ago, the playful, curious child was hurt and went into hiding. This pain is like a black hole in the center of her mind that she'll do anything to avoid. Betsy fears boredom, which she views as being unable to be entertained or distracted by anything at all. To her, this is a sign that she's slipping into depression.

In conversations Betsy often says, "It doesn't matter," but she really means, "I don't matter." Because she feels unimportant, she's learned to be an escape artist. In groups she's the least likely to let others know what's going on with her. She appears to be a good listener because she never interrupts or speaks. But she's often dissociated. She has suppressed the cheerful, energetic child who was rejected by her alcoholic parents. Instead she identifies with the frozen grief, sadness, and despair of feeling empty, meaningless.

Betsy's mask is a false self that identifies with the frozen memories of her early childhood experiences in a fear-based environment. Just as her parents did, Betsy keeps a lid on her happiness. As a child, nobody was there to comfort her grief when she discovered how easily the people you count on can disappear behind a closed door. Instead she learned that craving attention would bring humiliation. So she covers up her pain by appearing to attend to others. But Betsy remains disconnected because she's unable to meet her own emotional needs. To her, it feels safer to be hopeless than to risk connection, so she continually repeats the pattern and drains her life-force energy in the process. When depression takes over, she sometimes fantasizes about suicide. Her strategy, most of the time, was to try to import a false sense of happiness in the same way her parents did, with drugs and alcohol.

Because she was so good at hiding her needs, it took me a while to connect with Betsy. On my way to work one morning, I thought about her. There was something about her lack of energy that I found disturbing. A signal from my own tender heart was sending me a message. Pausing to listen to this signal, I realized that I was reacting to Betsy because she reminded me of a frozen part of myself that I was rejecting. Looking more closely, I flashed back to a period of my life when I too was trapped in the pit of depression.

Buddhist psychology has some words that cannot be translated into English. One of them is *bardo,* describing a dreamlike, disorganized tumble through space when the ground is pulled out from under you. This is the same concept as the yellow light. It's an expanded in-between state that can happen during any gap in your life, though in Buddhism it's traditionally associated with death. After graduating from high school I fell into this kind of psychological groundlessness, tossed around by intense fear and recklessness. Looking back, I was grappling with issues I was only barely aware of at the time. For several years I suffered from depression.

Reconnecting with this memory gave me a chance to surround that frozen part of my own experience with compassion. I remembered that recovering from my depression had a lot to do with addressing unresolved grief issues, and this opened my heart and helped me connect with Betsy. Using the positive interruption of empathy as a springboard, I asked Betsy if she would be willing to change the language we used, and talk about the core of her sadness as grief rather than despair. Her response was immediate. Normally she stared at the floor, but she looked up and our eyes met. Contact.

Having connected with the heart of her sadness, I found myself more able to notice other positive interruptions. Now and then little cracks in her persona would appear—quick moments when a twinkle returned to her eyes and the sunlight seemed to shine through. Whenever this happened, no matter how briefly, I made a point of mirroring that green light back to her. I had caught sight of the real Betsy, curious and awake and ready to come out of hiding.

By paying attention to these positive interruptions, I learned that one of Betsy's gifts to this world is her love of animals. She has a soft, playful side that comes out in the presence of any furry creature. In those relationships she could experience herself as open and unself-conscious. By building upon these positive qualities, Betsy was able to recover more and more confidence in her basic goodness and learn to trust the natural communication system of her awake body, tender heart, and open mind.

Because it is immediate, in the present moment, mindful communication is the language of our true nature, which has never been damaged by trauma nor limited by our negative ideas about who we are. Some systems of therapy focus on insight, while others increase compassion for the parts of ourselves that we've rejected. There are still other schools that bring us back into our bodies. Whatever route we take, if healing occurs, it is because we've reconnected with who we really are. Once we recognize this flash of the green light, we can stop identifying with the false protection of our red-light patterns and gain courage to investigate the groundlessness of our core fears and doubts. In this process, we shift our perspective from me-first to we-first as we let go of our projections and gain confidence in the authentic experience of our natural wakefulness.

SUMMARY OF MINDFUL-PRESENCE TRAINING

Go with the green light: Make the intention to be positively interrupted by flashes of wakefulness from body, heart, or mind.

When the light is red, stop: Set boundaries to prevent unnecessary distractions. To train in this, practice sitting meditation.

Be careful when the light is yellow: The core fear of the false self is the feeling of being cut off, unwelcome, depressed. Meet this fear and self-doubt with wakeful kindness.

3

The Key to Mindful Listening
Encouragement

To be aware of a single shortcoming within oneself is more useful than to be aware of a thousand in somebody else. Rather than speaking badly about people and in ways that will produce only friction and unrest in their lives, we should practice a purer perception of them, and when we speak of others, speak of their good qualities.

—THE DALAI LAMA

HIGH SCHOOL math teacher Jack Norton has a knack for bringing out the best in his students. "I love Mr. Norton's class a lot," says Chloe, who struggled in the past with math. "He has a great way of teaching, and somehow he makes each person feel valued. He tells us that everyone brings something special to the classroom. He cheers us on. And he's funny too."

The secret to Jack's approach is simple. He doesn't resort to phony praise or flattery with his students. Instead, he has a kind of X-ray vision that sees through their negative self-images. He tunes in to their unique qualities and brings these forward. This approach to communication is what Carl Rogers calls "uncon-ditional positive regard." It happens naturally when we pay attention with the presence of our awake body, the empathy of our tender heart, and the curiosity of our open mind. This is the key to mindful listening, the quality of encouragement.

Being able to listen attentively is the most important skill in communication. Encouragement amplifies that attention by warming it up with curiosity about each person's natural gifts. This, together with an enthusiasm for we-first vision, helps Jack's students see themselves as part of a larger whole. Jack sees virtues in his students that they don't recognize within themselves. So he makes a point of putting those observations into words.

"Amy, you are so amazingly creative. You're always discovering a new way of looking at the problem."

"Nico, I can always count on you to show up on time. You're so reliable and responsible. I really appreciate that."

The effect of Jack's encouragement is that each student feels nourished and valued and wants to live up to the excellence he envisions. At the same time, Jack also has a policy of "rewarding failure" by enthusiastically demonstrating the value of being open to learning through trial and error. "When we get the right answer, we're at a stopping point. But when we get the wrong answer, now we can get to work and have some fun! It's only by making mistakes that we can really learn something."

Jack leads by example, sharing his own vulnerable missteps openly and with humor. His approach creates a noticeable mood of cooperation, and it's obvious that his students are learning more than math in his classroom. They're learning how to create we-first systems by encouraging one another.

GARDENERS AND LIDS

An encouraging leader is like a gardener who can envision a flower in every seed and makes an effort to cultivate that potential in others. There is a generosity of spirit that comes with listening openly. We can afford to encourage others because we're drawing from a limitless supply of confidence. This confidence arises from being present with awake body, tender heart, and open mind. We all qualify as leaders whenever our conversations have the power to influence the social atmosphere around us. By listening mindfully and encouraging others we can build a culture of kindness in our families, workplaces, and communities.

While the encouraging leader is like a gardener, the discouraging leader is more like a lid. When we don't listen to one another, we contribute to an environment of paranoia and mistrust. When the light is red, cooperation changes into competitiveness. We don't want anyone to grow taller than we are.

Toxic Certainty

Lid-style leaders gain authority because they appear to never question their own positions. They have strong, unforgiving opinions about right and wrong. But unlike the natural confidence of the encouraging leader, this kind of doubtlessness and righteousness comes from a closed mind and heart. This toxic certainty is a red-light signal to watch out for. The term *toxic certainty* was used by author Wayson Choy to describe the platform of opinions that causes us to feel contempt for others. Toxic certainties mask our vulnerabilities and uncertainties by giving us a ground to stand on—a set of beliefs that build ourselves up by creating the illusion of superiority.

These platforms of toxic certainty are reinforced by the circles of influence around us—our family, workplace, friends, the media, social norms in general. One of the lessons to be learned from practicing mindful communication is the humble discovery of how easily any one of us can slip into these patterns of putting others down.

When mindlessness rules and we don't listen to one another

with warmth and curiosity, a negative culture takes root in our homes and communities. Discouraging conversations become normal. No one would deliberately say, "Let's get together for lunch and gossip about our mutual friends so that we'll end up feeling more mistrustful and unhappy." But when we don't pause and take a look at what we're doing, this is what can happen. When we're in a roomful of people who agree with our opinions, we get confused about what is true and what isn't. This is how toxic certainty takes root.

My teacher Sakyong Mipham Rinpoche advises us to be sensitive to the way our everyday conversations create these social environments: "In making friends, we are cultivating the influence of each other's view. If we want to rule our world, we need to be mindful about who we are hanging out with and aware of their influence."[1]

Seesaw Patterns of Flattery and Put-downs

Like the lid of a jar, an arrogant leader discourages people who come close to the ceiling of their own authority. They enlist someone for the role of "inferior" so that they can compare themselves and prove they are superior. Or vice versa. Another red-light signal in our communication is the seesaw pattern of flattery and put-downs. Flattery and put-downs are equally discouraging. The seesaw turns on comparisons that inflate ourselves at the expense of others. Since this pattern can be well disguised, investigate any instance when you compare yourself to others, either positively or negatively. The hidden message is that "my side is better than yours," a thin disguise for "I am better than you."

These comparisons hide themselves in our everyday communication and they plant the seeds of intolerance and contempt. For instance, one day I felt frustrated and threatened by a phone call from one of our grant administrators. During a lunch-hour walk with a colleague I said, "You and I are professionals, and we deserve some respect from these bureaucrats." Using labels to divide "us" from "them" was surprisingly effective. But my higher ground disappeared when I realized that I'd once again slipped into a red-light pattern, overvaluing myself at the expense of someone I thought of as inferior.

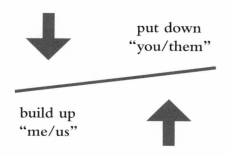

Fig. 2. See-Saw pattern.

DIFFERENT KINDS OF LISTENING

Listening is like pouring tea into a cup. When the cup is clean and empty, we're able to hear what the other person is saying clearly, and this is green-light listening. But when the conditions aren't in place, we can't listen and the light is red. One example of red-light listening is when the cup is upside down. This is when we have no interest at all in listening to the other person. Another example is when the teacup has a crack in it and the tea leaks out. This is when we're trying to listen but our attention is out of control. And the third example is when the teacup has something else in it already, which is what happens when we're full of toxic certainty. This is when we mix someone else's story with our own and edit the two together. When these red-light patterns are habitual, communication can be blocked for years.

It's surprising how often we think we're listening when we're not. For instance, in a counseling session I asked Pete to repeat back what his wife, Barb, had just said. Barb's words were, "I feel badly that we're late today."

Pete mirrored her this way: "What Barb said was that those damn tourists were all over the place this morning and they slowed down the traffic."

Barb looked at me and raised one eyebrow. This was an amusing example of red-light listening. Pete's teacup was already full.

Red-light listening indicates that communication is blocked. Because we can't listen, our response is inside out, more about *me* than anything else. We've become distracted from the conversation, or preoccupied by a thought or an idea or an emotional story line running through our mind, and we can't pay attention.

Unable to Be Heard: The Yellow-Light Crisis

What happens to our natural confidence and encouragement when the flow of communication is blocked? Discouragement sets in. To understand the roots of our own discouragement, it's important to pay close attention to what happens in our own hearts and minds at times like this. When the other person stops listening to us or misinterprets what we're saying, a kind of crisis takes place. In those eyes we've turned from a living human being into an object. When toxic certainty or putdowns are added to the conversation, we can easily be triggered to relive painful frozen memories. Most likely we'll scramble, trying to figure out what happened. This is that vulnerable time when our self-doubts surface. "What did I do wrong? Is there something wrong with me?"

I recently saw an example of this while riding the commuter train. A young mother was listening to her iPod through earphones while her toddler was excitedly looking out the window at the images flashing by. "Wazzat, Mama, wazzat!" he repeated over and over again. But his mother's attention was somewhere else. The little boy's initial joy turned into urgency: "Mama, Mama, wazzat, wazzat." Still no response. You could practically see his spirits collapse into a two-year-old version of despondency.

Because we human beings are relationship oriented, our sense of self is shaped by experiences like this little boy had on the train. We don't have to be two years old to feel an emotional impact when communication breaks down. But most of the time, like that little child, we don't have a way to understand what is happening. To prevent a toxic authority from seizing control of our mind, we need to open up a friendly dialogue with the confusion that surrounds our inner discouragement.

The Story of Ann: How to Use Three Lights

In the opening chapter I described how I noticed that, in my interactions with my coworker Robert, I tended to identify with whatever defensive mask I was wearing. But during that period in between being open and being closed, I felt unmasked and unsure of myself. At times like those I often stopped by the office of a good friend named Ann, who created a positive, encouraging space for me. The way she did this gave me some tips that I've adapted here to match the three slogans.

First of all, after mindfully listening, Ann would mirror back to me what I was saying, giving me the reassurance that I had been heard. "So what you're telling me is that you had a run-in this morning with Robert and you felt embarrassed because you didn't know how to stand up for yourself."

This first step is an example of how we apply the slogan "Go with the green light." Ann's mindful presence offered validation, or a reality check, on what I just said.

Secondly, Ann refrained from talking negatively about Robert. This is an example of how we apply the slogan "When the light is red, stop." If our conversation got misdirected onto Robert, we'd miss the point, which was to work directly with my own fear.

Then, in the third step, Ann would show her Midas touch,

going for the gold. She would rephrase my experience without distorting it, but play it back to me in a way that made my authentic qualities shine. "Susan, your love of harmony is a beautiful gift for this world. You long to connect with people in a genuine way. Like a little child holding a bouquet of flowers, offering this gift to Robert is nothing to be ashamed of. The pain of your embarrassment is like a wound from the past that you need to heal, not something negative."

The effect of even one conversation with Ann was transformative for me. The slogan "When the yellow light is flashing, be careful" means we need to protect these vulnerable conversations with mindful encouragement.

Here's a quick summary of these three steps:

1. *Go with the green light:* Reflecting like a mirror, to validate what you are hearing by repeating the words back.
2. *Stop at the red light:* Keep a we-first approach by refraining from harming someone's reputation.
3. *When the yellow light is flashing, be encouraging:* Replay the hidden gold in the story you heard by rewording it with unconditional positive regard.

Ann demonstrated to me that genuine confidence comes from humbleness, unmasking rather than putting on a front. She dissolved my need to prove I was superior to Robert as well as my fear that I was inferior to him. She helped me recover my own mindful presence so that I could be open and encouraging to others.

I described Ann's mindful encouragement as "going for the gold" because, like a miner, she could spot a sparkling nugget in my dark tunnel by listening with awake body, tender heart, and open mind. Like Jack, when she spotted the gold, she pointed to it. We need encouragement when things don't go as planned, because the feelings it exposes are so intimate. When I was feeling hurt, embarrassed, insulted, or irritated by Robert, I realized that my security system had failed. But Ann helped me see that this system was unnecessary in the first place. Because our true nature is we-first, we can't protect ourselves from being emotionally affected by other people. This so-called failure is good news for mindfulness practitioners. Those painful gaps in our defense systems enable us to realize that the sensitivity of our naked heart is more authentic than our masks.

Breaking the Spell

Machig Labdrön, a meditation master who lived in Tibet centuries ago, recommended that the best way to see through our fear-based self-images is to spend time in graveyards and other places that are haunted. In modern times, this idea sounds more like an invitation to a Halloween party. Today, the haunted areas that scare us are within our own minds. When things don't go as planned and we free-fall into the yellow-light zone, we lose confidence in ourselves. Negative voices in our mind sound like evil curses from the distant past coming back to haunt us: "You'll never amount to anything," "You're too fat to be lovable," "Lazy bum," "You didn't deserve her anyway," "Who do you think you are?" These are the discouraging prophesies of our inner toxic leader.

An encouraging listener such as Ann or Jack can challenge these curses and break the spell that they have over us. We do this for ourselves by mixing qualities like curiosity, gentleness, and presence with our fears and self-doubts. The best time to do this is when the yellow light is flashing and we're feeling vulnerable. This is an opportunity to go directly to the root of our false identity and establish an encouraging dialogue with those hidden "curses" that keep us afraid of who we are.

The slogan "Be careful when the yellow light is flashing" is a reminder that conversations, environments, and even the music we listen to can positively or negatively influence us when we're in the yellow zone. We need to be careful whom we talk to—and whom we listen to—when that background anxiety moves to the foreground. An encouraging friend can help us meet those fears and transform the grip they have on our sense of identity.

Practicing mindful listening, we learn to respond differently to yellow-light signals, welcoming the rejected parts of ourselves with compassionate insight. Mindful encouragement restores our intuitive wisdom so that we know how to respond appropriately. This is how we switch from prey to playmate. Like Churchill the dog, our intrinsic sanity tells us what we need to do, once we learn how to listen.

Gently Listening to Vulnerable Feelings

When we listen, sometimes we tune in to the green light, the naturally open and awake quality of our body, heart, and mind. At other times we listen to the red light, those negative voices that come along with physical and emotional tension. A third kind of listening is the in-between stage. We could call this "listening even though we're afraid of what we'll hear."

An encouraging listener can relate to fear because of the humble realization that all human beings suffer from similar misunderstandings. Seeing this, we use our sphere of influence for the benefit of others rather than to promote ourselves. Our confidence comes from having made a personal journey through the dark tunnel of our own self-doubt and discovering the sunlight of our true nature on the other side.

First we need to enter this tunnel—our own shadow world that amplifies the voice of our inner toxic leader. What are the negative influences, the unfriendly authorities within our mind that discourage us? We can notice these self-denigrating voices during yellow-light episodes, when the ground of our security falls out from under us.

For example, imagine you're walking out the door and suddenly realize you can't find your wallet. For the first few minutes of searching in the usual places, you're hopeful that it will show up, but after a little while an inner bully voice becomes audible. You start to blame your partner, convinced that she or he must have taken the wallet out of your pocket and left it lying around somewhere. You start feeling paranoid that someone's broken into your house. You panic about your boss's reaction to your being late. You start feeling a little crazy.

These small crises happen every day, causing our inner self-doubts to surface. During these in-between times, the predictable world we've created out of familiar reference points seems to fall apart. When we feel ungrounded like this, we're easily persuaded to lose confidence in ourselves. This is why we need to be careful and keep a close eye on the discouraging influences that affect us both in our external environment and within our own mind.

When fear rises up and we're not sure of ourselves, we can enlist the power of encouragement to dissolve the obstacles. Yellow-light listening gives us a chance to see our background anxieties surfacing while not completely losing touch with the person we're listening to. This is what happened to me in my conversation with Betsy. I was interrupted by emotional memories from my past. Temporarily, the focus shifted from we to me when I felt disconnected from her, distracted by an unrecognized projection of my own experience of depression. Then, by listening to this fear and reconnecting with my body, heart, and mind, I was able to recognize this projection and meet it with the compassion and insight that I gained from healing my depression. The pain that had been a barrier now became a bridge. It naturally shifted from me-first back into we-first. I was able to extend those qualities to Betsy with genuine confidence in her intrinsic sanity.

The key to listening deeply is to stay in touch with the messages coming to us from our body, heart, and open mind. What does our body feel like when the yellow light is flashing? What are the feelings that happen just before we shut down? Usually there is an abrupt surge in adrenaline as the fight-or-flight mechanism kicks in. Mindfully communicating with this fear in the body requires the delicate balance of letting it be while at the same time not letting it run away with us. To do that we need to ventilate with fresh air. So, it's important to breathe. Bringing our attention to the body and to our breathing, we come back to the present moment, creating space to allow our pain to express itself, like a wounded animal. Breathing, we surround this feeling with acceptance, responding like a loving friend or parent.

The toxic patterns in our communication can be traced back to a false system of trying to protect ourselves from fear and pain. But we unwittingly end up amplifying both. The mindfulness practice of deep listening encourages us to be curious about this pain. With gentle curiosity, we touch the pain directly and learn new, more effective ways of taking care of ourselves. Opening to the physical pain in our body also opens us to all the other pain in our lives. By penetrating our defensive barriers with mindfulness, we can learn to hold this pain like a newborn baby, gently but protectively. As my teacher says, the mind of fear needs to be placed in a cradle of loving-kindness.

Paul, Sheila, and Mia

Any one of us can create a culture of kindness in our lives by listening deeply to our own communication patterns and learning to be more encouraging. Here's an example from the Baxter family. Paul and Sheila and their teenage daughter, Mia, came to me for counseling because they were in conflict about Mia's curfew on Saturday nights. A crisis had erupted the previous week when Mia didn't come home at all, claiming she'd spent the night with a girlfriend because she was afraid of her dad's anger. I introduced them to the concept of the three lights, and we listened carefully to three different ways that anger was manifesting in this family.

CLOSED COMMUNICATION

Paul was furious and mistrustful, with a closed-communication stance, firmly believing the only option was that Mia should be punished. His anger had turned heartless, and he was displaying the kind of toxic certainty we discussed earlier. He justified his rigid position by saying he was a strong father. When I asked him how he might visualize this strength, he said it was like a dam holding back the flood that could sweep away his family. He loved his daughter and his wife, but he realized their relationships were eroding. He believed that grounding Mia—which he called, "giving her consequences"—was a way of protecting her. This approach may have had some merit if she were younger and if there'd been no hidden agenda. But as he continued to speak, it became more evident that Paul wanted to retaliate against her for challenging his authority.

THE ALARM SIGNALS OF HEALTHY ANGER

Sheila's response to the family crisis could be more accurately labeled "alarm" than anger, because while the sense of urgency was there—her face was hot and her heart was pounding—her focus was not self-centered. This is an example of how green-light anger alerts us to a problem that needs to be solved.

In the past, Sheila had her own version of the red light. Using a mindless pattern, she tried to manage Paul's aggression by suppressing what she knew to be true: that her daughter was being hurt by the communication breakdown.

After listening to Paul and Sheila, I realized that we needed to set up a protection for Mia before inviting her to speak. I introduced the slogan "Stop when the light is red" to recognize when two-way communication has stalled. When this happens, I told them, I would hold up my hand to pause. This was a signal for the green-light partner to either be silent or to practice reflective listening.

Paul resumed by saying, "If I give her an inch, she'll take a mile."

"Listen to yourself," Sheila replied. "What do you think it's like to be at the receiving end of a comment like that? It's so impersonal to talk to her that way. You are making a prediction that puts Mia in a no-win position. When you tell her that rules are rules, you're saying and doing the very things that push Mia away."

As long as Paul's light was red, the conversation could go no farther. But something shifted for Paul when he heard Sheila rephrasing his words back to him. Later he described a sadness that was held in his body like a clenched fist. His rigid beliefs had given him the illusion of control over life's challenges. But now he was feeling powerless and bewildered. It was wonderful to see his emotional light change from red to yellow as he began to let go of solid ground and eventually started listening to his daughter.

FEELING VULNERABLE

Mia had been sitting silently during the conversation, staring at the floor with her arms crossed. She'd felt hurt and frustrated by her father's opinions, and very angry as a result, as if reduced to an object by his generalizations. He seemed to have no interest in listening to her true experience. This is an example of yellow-light anger, the shaky in-between zone of feeling vulnerable and at risk of shutting down. Mia tearfully blurted out, "You don't really care about what happens to me! You don't love anyone but yourself and your stupid rules!"

I asked Paul and Sheila if I could have a conversation with Mia in front of them, without being interrupted. Then I asked Mia to talk more about what her values were, what she considered to be dangerous behavior, and to describe what kind of protection she needed. Mia prefaced her comments by saying that she wished her dad realized how disciplined she was, that she knew there were lots of kids in her high school who were experimenting with drugs, sex, alcohol and tobacco, "and lots of other things," but that she wasn't interested. "It all depends on who you hang out with," she said. "My friends are not like that."

By listening to Mia, Paul felt his opinions giving way and his heart softening. Internally, a courageous process was taking place. He was detaching from the voice of toxic certainty, which was his father's voice, and opening to a part of himself that reminded him of his daughter. He was reconnecting with the quality of unconditional friendliness for himself, enabling him to see Mia more clearly. Feeling the pain in his body and the sadness in his heart, he was learning to hold steady, breathe, and allow his experience to simply be here, in the present moment.

When asked to talk more about what it would mean to let go of the possessive grip he had on Mia, Paul began to talk about his own childhood. He had been a naturally curious child who loved to explore. He painfully remembered how his joy in learning came to a full stop when he met his own father's red light. The word *mistake* took on an ominous meaning. To avoid punishment and ward off any danger of being caught making a mistake, Paul took refuge in rules. As long as there were rules, there was someone to blame. The false protection of Paul's rigid belief system, which had formed in childhood due to the influence of his punishing father, gave way to a more effective kind of protection.

Paul's fear that mistakes were unforgivable was a frozen memory. By learning to listen to himself more openly, he was able to revisit this memory in a new way. In a subsequent session I gave Paul an audio recording of a guided meditation to take home. Here are some excerpts:

> This is the time to become you own loving father. That means going in the opposite direction. Instead of going with your thoughts, connect directly to the pain that you're feeling, without trying to adjust the facts to soften

the blow. Hold steady and go directly into the feelings held in your body. Where are they? What do they feel like? Now listen to the voice of that toxic leader, the voice that tells you that you've committed an unforgivable crime. Do you really believe this? Do you really believe you should be perfect? Does this mean that all mistakes are punishable? Now it's time to surround that pain with compassion. You need to interrupt that irrational thinking with another voice, the voice of a true friend.

In my office, over the next few weeks, the green-light conversations between Mia and her parents continued, and their relationships became more flexible and resilient.

Furthermore, when Paul and Sheila engaged with each other in this new way, the tension in the family began to resolve. The culture of toxic authority was transforming into a culture of kindness. They entered into family dialogues with Mia on the topic of trust. Listening to his daughter, Paul realized that Mia didn't need the kind of protection he was trying to give her, which she described as being "like keeping me in a prison to make me safe." What Mia needed was to be seen and heard for who she was, a young woman with a strong inner sense of direction and good judgment. When communication in the family opened up again, Mia began asking her dad's advice from time to time, reminding him that although she was becoming more independent, she still needed a father to look up to.

There is a saying that you cannot hate someone once you know his or her story. The antidote to our toxic certainties comes from openly listening and being curious to learn more about one another. When we listen to our stories, they unfold from the tight knot of our opinions into a more tender story about the experiences we've had in our lives. By listening deeply and openly like this, we replace the inner toxic authority figures in our own mind with a more loving, nurturing leader and reconnect with our genuine nature. Turning points sometimes manifest very abruptly when this happens.

JOURNAL EXERCISE: VOICES THAT DISCOURAGE AND ENCOURAGE

- Create a welcoming environment so that you can deeply listen to yourself.
- What are the toxic certainties that discourage you? Where did these come from? How do they make you feel?
- Create an inner dialogue between the toxic leader and an encouraging voice.
- Describe the qualities in yourself that you previously were unable to see.

THREE KINDS OF EMOTIONS

In the conversations with Paul, Sheila, and Mia, we saw that the feeling of anger manifested in three different ways in this family: red, green and yellow. This is a helpful technique in mindful-communication training. Some emotions are open, others are closed, and some are in-between. When we're open, our emotional intelligence is a source of encouragement, offering intuitive information about the other person or about what needs to happen in the situation. But when we're closed, our emotions can turn toxic. Keeping our finger on the emotional pulse of the conversation helps us notice when we get distracted by our own issues or projections.

Open, Green-Light Emotions

Green-light emotions are a range of tender we-first responses such as compassion, joy, love, and sadness. We tune in to emotional messages, as if we were hearing the melody behind the lyrics of a song. These responses are always appropriate to the situation because they aren't centralized or generated by our internal stories. They arise spontaneously with events in the external environment. For instance, Sheila's anger functioned like an alarm going off in the family system, alerting her to the problem with Paul's toxic authority that was harming all three of them.

All green-light emotions, even anger, are essentially expressions of empathy. They arise when we listen with an open heart, feeling as one with the joy and pain of other people. These poignant feelings enable us to smile in response to beauty—a spring flower, a crescent moon. We cry when we learn about human suffering in wars or natural disasters, such as floods, tornadoes, or tsunamis. Because they are naturally "we-first," green-light emotions tune us in to the "gold" in other people, the unique qualities and gifts they have to offer. When we witness injustice or see the goodness in people being suppressed, empathic anger can empower us to move beyond our comfort zone for the well-being of others.

Green-light emotions are intelligent and appropriate responses to the events in our environment. They arise before we divide our experience into me and you. They are the energies of relationship that sometimes function to cut through obstacles whereas at other times they draw in the energy we need. They are raw human experience, the joy of falling in love, the grief of death, or the spontaneous generosity of rescuing a stranger in distress.

The defining characteristic of green-light emotions is that they do not cause harm, even though they can be painful. For instance sometimes in a relationship, a burst of anger might clear the air and open up communication that has become blocked or stale. It rises up like a flame appearing out of a wooden match, sharp and brilliant, and then it fizzles out when the conditions change. If it stays in the present moment and doesn't turn into resentment or hatred, this emotional energy is green-light.

Key points about green-light emotions:

- They are fluid and responsive to our natural communication system: open-hearted, synchronized with body and mind.
- They are intelligent ways of knowing.
- They are expressions of the present moment.
- They are naturally we-first, responsive to the needs of relationship.
- They inform us about what to do.
- They make things better the more we listen to them.

Closed, Red-Light Emotions

Red-light emotions are forms of discouragement that result from communication shutdown. They take over our mind, like a hostile leader, and block our ability to listen to new information in the present moment. They are generated by fearful thoughts about the past and the future rather than by information from now. They create all kinds of unnecessary suffering, above and beyond the unavoidable pain of ordinary life.

Paul's aggressive anger was a red-light emotion. These negative emotions feel overwhelming at times because they endlessly spin off from our thoughts and aren't grounded in reality. Depression is like a five-hundred-pound bully sitting on our chest, crushing any sense of hope. Anxiety never gives us a moment of peace. Craving is like a drug pusher, constantly trying to hook us. The seesaw reactions of contempt and self-importance are like living in a high-maintenance mansion that needs constant surveillance. Envy eats away at us, pushing us to compete because the fear of being a loser is unthinkable.

When we practice mindfulness, we observe that these toxic emotions have no basis in reality. A clue is that they never occur when we're open. They are also noticeably absent in enlightened masters, saints, and people of great character whom we admire. This is because red-light feelings are conditioned responses. They may be familiar and habitual, but they aren't essential to human nature. So they are more analogous to a costume than to our skin. These feelings only arise when communication is closed. They are triggered by mental fiction rather than by fact.

Red-light emotions are forms of mindlessness. They ignore our interdependent root system and cause us to react as if relationship doesn't matter. They spin off from a negative view of ourselves and then try to protect it with the cocoon of "me-first." Feeling cut off keeps us emotionally hungry and defensive.

The good news for mindful communicators is that the scripts for our red-light emotions are easily recognized in our conversations if we listen for them. The trouble is that when the light is red, we don't want to listen to ourselves. Practicing mindfulness meditation transforms these secondary emotions by interrupting our thought processes and returning us to nowness, over and over again. We realize that red-light emotions are always an effort to block fear. When we stay present, refraining from acting them out or suppressing them, we are one step closer to understanding this fear.

Key points about red-light emotions:

- They are frozen patterns created by thoughts and mental scripts.
- They are felt in the body as tension.
- They focus on past and future rather than staying with the first moment.
- They cause harm when not recognized.
- They are not true—they originate from inner fictions, not external reality.
- They have the view of "me-first" or "win-lose".
- They make things worse the more we listen to them.
- The examples: hatred, jealousy, contempt, addictive craving, depression.

Vulnerable, Yellow-Light Emotions

Mia's anger was the frustration of feeling hurt and mistrusted by her father. Feeling hurt, disappointed, embarrassed, irritated, or insulted are just a few of the fear-based emotions associated with the yellow light. They are triggered when things don't go as planned, causing a breach in our security system. Normally we try to quickly suppress these vulnerable emotions, because we fear they indicate that something is wrong with us. They might prove we're unlovable, unworthy, unforgivable, unwelcome, powerless. Instead of investigating these fears we cover them with a mask, the false identity we come to believe is "me."

Defensiveness is like a security guard for our false identity, trying to protect us by keeping our attention away from those painful self-images. Instead, we learn to live with the background anxiety of our core fears and self-doubts.

A yellow-light emotion begins with a little jolt—the shock and disorientation that comes when we realize we're out of step with reality. It's as if you're driving along a mountain highway on a brilliant summer day and then unexpectedly find yourself in a dark tunnel. Sudden groundlessness includes a whole range of vulnerable feelings that flare up when something unexpected comes out of nowhere.

Yellow-light emotions are linked with frozen memories from periods in our life when we didn't have enough compassionate support to cope when we lost connection to a significant person. When we try to push away pain or fear, it becomes a background anxiety, like an alarm that won't shut off. The physical and emotional energy of anxiety maintains the secret fear that "something is wrong with me."

Like the secondary emotions of the red light, the energy of yellow-light emotions is mixed up with confused ideas. Unlike the red-light emotions, these ideas are not scripted into complete story lines. They remain fragments of self-doubt that we

THREE KINDS OF EMOTIONS

GREEN LIGHT:	RED LIGHT:	YELLOW LIGHT:
We-First	Me-First	Doubt
Alarm	Aggression	Frustration
Sadness	Depression	Disappointment
Love/Appreciation	Craving	Emotional Hunger
Empathy	Anxiety	Fear
Joy	Intoxication/Mania	Embarassment
Compassion	Jealousy	Guilt
Admiration	Contempt	Insult

try to ignore. Instead of responding to the present moment, these fragments of fear contribute to a background sense of being cut off from ourselves.

Instead of facing this fear directly, we continue to seek solutions in other people. This is the sad irony that leads to so much of our suffering in relationships. The very struggle to distance from our own fear is exactly what creates the fear in the first place.

Let's review a few of the qualities of openness and then notice what being cut off from them is like:

- A sense of connection becomes the feeling of being cut off.
- Unconditional acceptance becomes rejection of certain parts of our experience.
- Genuine confidence becomes an inner feeling of unworthiness covered up by self-importance.
- Our capacity to love becomes the fear that we're unlovable, the hunger to be loved.
- Natural responsiveness becomes impulsive or compulsive actions based on a feeling of powerlessness.

During the years I taught programs on nonviolence, I introduced the idea that the energy of our sensitive emotions is like the weather. Many of my clients were fishermen and hunters, people who knew the importance of being able to tell when a storm was coming. Ignoring the weather report can lead to disaster. I explained that when we feel hurt, disappointed, embarrassed, or insulted, it is as if our boat has capsized in turbulent waters. Because we didn't know how to listen to the weather report of our green-light emotions, we headed out to sea with unrealistic expectations, which caused us to overreact when things didn't go as planned. These clients perked up when they realized that it was possible to learn to read their own emotional weather reports more accurately. Drawing from their personal lives, they easily began to remember examples of emotional shipwrecks that could have been prevented.

Key points about yellow-light emotions:

- They are felt in the body as fear.
- They arise when things don't go as planned.
- They make us feel vulnerable, so we want to suppress them.
- They bring our hidden self-doubts to the surface.
- They are triggered by unrealistic expectations or when the communication barrier suddenly appears in a conversation.
- They can make one feel insulted, frustrated, hurt, irritated, worried, embarrassed, ashamed, bored.

CREATING A GREEN ZONE FOR OURSELVES

In my workshops, we acknowledge the transformative power of openness by using the term "green zone" to describe the time and place we create to allow genuine dialogue to take place. This includes the time we give ourselves for meditation, contemplation, creating art or music, or writing in our journal. Some of us think of a green zone as a sanctuary from war, while others associate it with protecting natural wilderness. These impressions are helpful because in some ways our personal green zones are both. A green zone is a gentle conversation that encourages sensitive yellow-light feelings to emerge. It is what author and educator Parker Palmer calls a "welcoming space" where we can speak our own truth and listen in such a way that we welcome the truth of other. Here we can let our guard down because protective boundaries are present. Those boundaries are created when we agree to stop at the red light, refraining from the kind of negative speech and distracted listening that contribute to a culture of fear.

When we feel hurt or emotionally wounded in an unfriendly environment, it's easy to become defensive, pushing people away. But mindfulness practice is a green zone, giving us the courage to listen to these subtle messages to find out what we really need. This enables us to recognize the way our vulnerable emotions express themselves so that we can recognize and respond to our needs.

Listening to Our Body

Reinhabiting our bodies allows pain and tension to simply be there so that we can listen and respond compassionately to the tender emotions we find there. To awaken communication with the energy within our body, we need to learn the language of our body's distress signals. For example, "My neck is so tight, it feels like there is a noose around it." Listening to this message, we might intuitively understand this to be a coded message that translates, "When I feel like crying, I'm afraid of looking stupid, so I suppress my pain by tightening my neck muscles."

Imagine the clear light of open mind moving through the body like a CT scan machine, accommodating whatever we find. Give the body room to express itself in its own language. Our body speaks to us in a language of contrast: hot or cold, clenching or release, pleasure or discomfort. To learn this language, we need to be curious about how our body signals to us that we're open, closed, or in-between. What does our body feel like when the light is green? When we're open, the synchronization of body, heart, and mind is our communication system with the environment around us, which we described in chapter 2. Mindfully listening to the messages that come from our body, we respond by meeting our body's needs: when we're tired, we sleep. When we're thirsty, we drink water.

When the light is red, we're out of touch with what we really need. For instance, our body is thirsty but our mind edits this message with a TV commercial. So instead of water we drink a soda or a beer. We suppress sensitive emotions by locking their energy tightly in our body armor, like a bud in winter. It might feel like a very long time before it softens. At first glance, the hard nubs of tension in our body seem unworkable. In an unfriendly environment, they can't soften. To work with suppressed emotions, we have to learn how to listen with self-acceptance and encouragement. Mindful listening identifies the inner voices that criticize and blame, and in the process we simply make room to feel the pain of being disconnected. When spring sunshine warms the branches of a tree, even the toughest buds begin to open.

Developing Encouragement by Listening with Open Mind

Training in mindfulness enables us to notice when we open and close. In meditation practice we notice gaps in our daydreams, as if we've set a mental alarm to wake up and gently return to the present moment. We do this by reconnecting to our breath. Training in mindful listening works with distractions in a similar way, bringing us back to the present moment and reconnecting us to the person with whom we're communicating. Using the breath and the awake posture of body is one support for this. Another is to ask for the speaker's help: "I'm sorry, I was having a hard time following you. Would you mind saying that again?" It also helps to use active listening skills such as mirroring back what we've heard or paraphrasing the ideas into our own words. Together, the speaker and listener can find the right balance in order to optimize the opportunity to get the message across.

Working with Seesaw Mind: Leveling the Playing Field

As an antidote to the seesaw pattern of comparisons (see fig. 2 on page 53), we need to level the playing field. Toxic leadership is gained by rewarding people with flattery and punishing them with criticism. Here's a contemplation my teacher gave me: If the praise is true, it doesn't matter. Praise doesn't add anything to our qualities or achievements. If the praise is not true, it is only flattery and doesn't mean anything. So let it go. If the criticism is true, then it's helpful feedback that we can use. If it's not true, then it is only a projection from the other person, and means nothing. Working with this contemplation is one way that we can distance ourselves from praise or criticism.

Another way to level the playing field and interrupt the seesaw effect is to listen for things we have in common with other people, rather than scanning for the ways we're better or worse. In my training as a mindfulness-based therapist we were warned to be careful of closed communication patterns that mask self-inflation as "professionalism." The challenge is to observe the points in our conversation where we distance ourselves from our client's experience, as I did with Betsy. When this happens, we abandon the we-first relationship and turn our client into an object. A therapist is in the role of leader or mentor. This doesn't mean we have to be perfect, but it is essential that we know jthe difference between our red-light projections—signals that we've closed down—and the bridge of empathy that connects us to our client. So every therapeutic relationship is a mutual journey of self-discovery.

Norman was a member of a long-term group therapy program that I supervised in a maximum-security prison. He was a large, flamboyant man with a red face and a tidy beard that made him look like a character out of a Shakespeare play. He had a natural gift for leadership, but he misused it to inflate himself rather than to encourage others. He came across as so confident in himself that people believed whatever he said even when they knew full well that he was making some of it up. He was a successful salesman.

Observing him in the group, I was awed by Norman's skill in using the seesaw pattern of flattery and put-downs to manipulate people. He kept the upper hand by pretending to be the authority on everything and never admitting that he needed help. He mixed criticism with a stinging wit when he put people down and then turned the blame on them if they called him on it. He was truly a master at defending himself as he blocked most opportunities for genuine communication.

Norman positioned himself so that people would look up to him, reminding him of his importance. The domain he created was a fear-based culture, and the economy was an exchange of flattery. In the middle of his circle, he was like a king in his castle, looking down on the peasant folk. The flashing yellow light that was sure to trigger Norman was the experience of being insulted. It showed his Achilles' heel: the core fear that under his suit of armor he had no value at all. Inner poverty can swallow us up when the balloon of our self-inflation pops. We can plunge from the castle into a moat of discouragement. The red zone of false pride is the opposite of genuine confidence. It's the need to be special, and it rejects the fear of being ordinary, which is associated with worthlessness.

Norman projected his fear of inadequacy onto others, whom he regarded with contempt. When I reflected on this, I remembered something I learned from my mindfulness teacher: generosity is the antidote to self-importance, because hoarding all qualities for ourselves is a form of stinginess. We hold on to any glittering object or circumstance that comes our way and keep it in our treasure chest as proof that we are special. Money, beauty, intelligence, academic standing—we don't want to share anything of value by seeing qualities in people outside our own ego domain.

The inner tug-of-war in Norman's personality was special-ness versus inferiority. This is what played itself out when he assumed leadership of the group. He needed to be an expert, an authority, to be looked up to. At first I couldn't find any ground for relating to Norm except to think of him as the opposite of myself, since I struggled so much with self-doubt. But then it occurred to me that while he was looking down on everyone else, I was looking down on him. A voice in my mind was stroking my own narcissism by judging him. I realized that I was afraid of falling under his power, that I too was susceptible to being controlled by praise and criticism.

Looking further, I saw that the ground I had in common with Norm was the fear of unworthiness. What if I was found out to be a fraud, a therapist who couldn't help? Suddenly I realized that my mask of professionalism was like his mask of being Mr. Know-It-All. I chuckled at the idea of Mr. and Mrs. Don't-Know-Anything engaged in a power struggle for the control of this group.

I remembered an incident when my mask of professionalism was pulled off. A few years earlier I'd traveled to Sitka, Alaska, to attend a weeklong training on traditional First Nations healing practices. I felt self-conscious about being a white therapist in the midst of a Native group. Then the trainer put me on the spot. Our inhibitions having been perceptively sized up, each of us was given an opposite role to act out. I was told to show up that afternoon as Tina Turner and sing "Proud Mary" for the group.

Terrified, I accepted the challenge. It was late October and during the lunch break I found a wig in the Halloween supplies section of a dollar store. I transformed a black shawl into a miniskirt. That afternoon I nervously put my outfit together in the small bathroom next to the auditorium where the group waited. At the last moment, I grabbed a highlighter pen to use as a fake microphone. When I stepped into the circle, the music blared and I let go.

I danced and pranced across the imaginary stage the way I'd done as a teenager in the privacy of my room with my Janis Joplin records. Now, in public, I was swirling and dancing and passionately belting my heart out in a song I hardly knew. Everyone was shocked to see this other side to my personality, and so was I. But somehow I made it through this rite of passage, and afterward there were no barriers left in our group.

Being willing to be a fool can be the perfect medicine when you're caught up in self-importance. It's good to laugh, have fun, and relax. Genuineness cuts through the fear that we are basically bad, or shameful. Instead we see our own goodness reflected back to us. What I remembered about this experience of unmasking was how important it was to have a trusting environment when you feel like a fool. I realized that with Norman I had to play with him a little bit, but be prepared to offer respect and gentleness whenever he began being honest with himself.

Norman was a Vietnam veteran. His mask had been frozen in place when his brother was killed during boot camp. He locked his vulnerable grief deep within him along with the memories of the war.

When Norm talked about this in a group session, one of the other men leaned forward. Bob was an older man who had come a long way over the past few months. He was also an AA sponsor and had learned a lot about the "stinking thinking" of denial and rationalization. He said softly, "Man, you don't need to carry that around for the rest of your life. That war kicked the daylight out of you. I know, I was there. But holding all that in is trauma, not courage."

There was a long, uncomfortable silence. The fluorescent lights buzzed overhead, and you could hear the distant echo of clanging prison doors down the hall. Norm's face began to tighten with rage as he glared at Bob. His fists clenched, and he half rose out of his chair. He paused, rigid as a statue. Then, out of nowhere, he fell back into his chair and began to sob. We sat in silence as he wept uncontrollably for several minutes, his whole body heaving. Finally the words came. He described how powerless he'd felt to help his brother. After a long pause, he started to talk again. There was nothing he'd been able to do but freeze and become like a statue wearing a uniform, he said.

Once he began to let these imaginary demons out, Norm took a deep sigh of relief. All the punishment in the world couldn't equal the self-hatred Norman inflicted on himself for those dark times. When Norman broke down, the other group members were ready to come forward and remind him not to define himself by the past. They repeated back one of our re-covery slogans: "Remember that our masks are not who we really are." The false self is a costume we can step out of; we can change our ways.

The group gave Norman's fall a soft landing, preventing him from becoming overwhelmed by self-recrimination. In the garden-like community we were creating, the essential goodness of each member was being cultivated above all else. When genuine remorse came up, we had to meet it with com-passion. At that point, recovery is possible, even in the most degraded of conditions. The compliments we gave Norman on his courage were clearly different from the kind of praise he normally craved. Seeing something true in his character was inviting an atmosphere of dignity and respect.

Seeing through Our Own Masks

The two basic scripts for red-light emotions are "heartless mind" and "mindless heart," which we'll discuss in more detail in chapters 4 and 5. Heartless mind aggressively pushes away the people and situations that seem threatening to us. Mindless heart craves emotional nourishment at all costs. These two scripts generate other secondary emotions, including jealousy, contempt, and despair. Out of nowhere, a trickster in our mind triggers a false alarm whenever we feel threatened or needy. Once the action movie in our mind is under way, we rarely pause to investigate if the script is true. We tend to take off in our usual direction, either acting out or suppressing the emergency reaction that's been triggered. That basic pattern is what freezes our natural green-light emotional intelligence into secondary, red-light emotions that cause trouble.

Not being able to pay attention keeps our red-light patterns in place. Like the little boy saying "Wazzat, Mama," we repeat the same story or opinion over and over again because we don't feel heard. The repetition goes on in our mind and in our conversations. The false self identifies with these mental obsessions, and we defend our opinions and beliefs so firmly that anyone who disagrees with us becomes an enemy. We've forgotten that our original longing was for connection, for a listening partner who would simply be present for us.

Open mind makes us curious about the stories we're hearing. This is the investigation aspect of mindful listening, asking questions to unravel the layers of the narrative we're hearing about. When we're listening openly, there is no solid "me" at the center of our awareness. Yet there is an inner space of solitude that holds us steady. This space is accommodating and curious, but also warm. What we call tender heart is inseparable from this open space.

Open mind is nondualistic, like the natural landscape. It is how we experience our lives directly, before the landscape becomes artificially divided into territories of "me" and "you" that cause us to go to war. To illustrate this in my workshops, I sometimes point to a wall map and say, "Here are all these nations with clear boundaries that human beings are willing to die for. But when you're out there in the bush, can you find these dividing lines carved into the landscape? They are created by ideas and agreements, but those lines aren't real."

The power of encouragement is the ability to see the heart of gold in one another, because we've found it in ourselves. It builds confidence in the inherent goodness of human nature. It makes us more tolerant of one another, because we know that the unseen forces of mindlessness are based on fear. It feels sad to see how futile it is to keep trying to meet our own needs by becoming heartless and mindless. We develop the power to genuinely encourage others by meeting our own self-doubts with kindness. We don't lose sight of our green-light vision: the masks and stories we cling to are not who we really are.

When we feel the sadness of disconnection, we need to surround this pain with a new understanding and lots of gentleness. We need to encourage the heart of gold to come forward. With the power of mindfulness we can discover that the fear-based self isn't truly solid. It appears out of nowhere whenever the light turns red. By training ourselves to stop when communication shuts down, we can bring loving attention to the misunderstandings and fears that trigger these defensive reactions.

The leader who is like a gardener, which we discussed earlier in this chapter, sees our true nature as basically good. The masks of defensiveness we wear come from fear, reinforced when we hang out with the wrong crowd. Using the power of encouragement we can create families and communities that flourish through gentleness. Instead of buying into the stories based on shame and self-doubt, we can arouse some curiosity about these core fears and feel compassion for those parts of ourselves that have been wounded and in hiding for so long.

4

The Key to Mindful Speech
Gentleness

When we're putting up the barriers and the sense of "me" as separate from "you" gets stronger, right there in the midst of difficulty and pain, the whole thing could turn around simply by not erecting barriers; simply by staying open to the difficulty, to the feelings that you're going through; simply by not talking to ourselves about what's happening. That is a revolutionary step. Becoming intimate with pain is the key to changing at the core of our being—staying open to everything we experience, letting the sharpness of difficult times pierce us to the heart, letting these times open us, humble us, and make us wiser and more brave. Let difficulty transform you. And it will. In my experience, we just need help in learning how not to run away.

—PEMA CHÖDRÖN

IN JANUARY 2009, Dr. Izzeldin Abuelaish, a Palestinian doctor who lives in the Gaza Strip, was interviewed shortly after an Israeli rocket blasted into his home and killed three of his daughters, his brother, and a nephew. He became famous for his response: "If I could know that my daughters were the last sacrifice on the road to peace between Palestinians and Israelis, then I would accept their loss."

We get a clue about Dr. Abuelaish's strength of character from Dr. Marek Glezerman, an Israeli doctor who described his friend's habit of choosing his words carefully: "Izzeldin doesn't generalize the way most of us do . . . [he] directs his anger in a focused way, never spreading it wide and letting the anger overwhelm and distract him from where he should be going."[1]

It's hard enough to speak mindfully under normal circumstances, but it is truly remarkable when we're able to hold steady during a painful moment. When the best of our intentions are overwhelmed, the slogan "When the light turns red, stop" can remind us that there is a difference between the raw, unavoidable distresses of life—primary experiences—and the unnecessary suffering created by mindless reactions. Becoming intimate with pain as well as with our negative reactions helps us be willing to transform our speech into gentleness.

Speaking gently increases the chances that what we say will be heard. By refraining from exaggerations or generalizations we can maintain a we-first perspective when we're angry or in pain. Speaking our truth is tricky. Mindfulness practice helps us investigate our motivations for expressing ourselves. Are we engaged in a "two-way-street" conversation or do we shut down the traffic with a one-way broadcast? Mindfulness shows us that everything we say is colored by our unique perceptions, our interpretations, and our emotional reactions. Recently, when a twenty-four-hour news TV network opened in Canada, a local journalism professor effectively asked, "How much of this information is news and how much is opinion?" This is the question we ask ourselves when we're practicing mindful speech.

Speaking gently isn't about being "nice," suppressing our rough edges like a naughty child. That kind of niceness turns our aggression inward in a mindless-heart style. Real gentleness comes from knowing that curiosity and empathy are more reliable defenses than opinion and reactivity. It comes from knowing that we need to protect our sense of connectedness, our relationships, rather than put up barriers around our personal territory. Our natural communication system is subtle, like the pulse a physician reads by holding a firm but light touch on our wrist. We feel this pulse with awake body, tender heart, and open mind. Staying open, even in conflict, allows communication to flow both ways. Gentleness tracks the pulse of the relationship, informing us of the effect our words are having on our listeners.

When communication breaks down, defensiveness overrules this intuitive connection. Aggression depends on self-deception. It tricks us into regarding red-light strategies as sources of power even though they wreak havoc with our life. When I reflected upon my communication with Robert, my coworker, it became clear that defensiveness was like a big neon target identifying me as the perfect prey. Sometimes I'd try on a mask of false confidence with him, pretending he meant nothing to me. But then I felt even more vulnerable, like the proverbial emperor with no clothes. False confidence only increased my sensitivity to Robert's insults. Occasionally, I even attempted a more openly aggressive defense by tackling the hungry bear head-on, and I'd get into an argument with him. But going to war only escalated the situation. In the long run, there were no winners. In spite of my motivation to be brave, I mostly just felt hurt or angry. With the benefit of hindsight, I could finally observe how my red-light strategies had failed me.

We need to remember that barriers to communication cut us off not only from others but also from ourselves. The way red-light reactions feel in our body is a kind of shutting down. Our physical energy is locked in our muscles. Our awareness of the environment shrinks as our sense perceptions are filtered into "me-first": what "I want" and what "I don't want." It feels as though our heart is closing. These are signals we can look for.

To practice mindful speech, it's important to understand how we turn heartless and mindless.

Shutting down when we're in pain is such a powerful habit that it feels instinctive. But the impulse to shut down only makes pain worse. The same thing is true in our communications with others. Because we don't know how to care for our emotional pain with gentle attention, it becomes inflamed, and then a secondary reaction sets in. Mindless anger turns into aggression, just like a neglected wound that gets infected.

Aggressive strategies deflect our attention away from pain by causing us to overreact or underreact. We try to discharge the irritation outward, blaming others, or else suppress it inward, blaming ourselves. The way to interrupt these aggressive strategies is by applying the slogan "When the light turns red, stop." We need to pause and take a closer look at all the ways we complicate our situation by exaggerating or suppressing our discomfort. Gentleness is discovered in between the primary energy of anger and the secondary, aggressive reactions that anger can trigger.

To transform aggressive communication patterns into gentleness, we first treat the infection, and then we relate to the original pain. This is the slow process of developing what my teacher calls "disciplined patience." The good news is that failure is necessary. It is impossible to build our immunity to infections in a completely sterile environment. We need to bump up against hostility—our own and others'—in order to learn patience.

Peacemakers train by thoroughly understanding the causes of war. Doctors train to stop infections by studying bacteria under a microscope. In the same way, mindful communicators train to protect relationships by observing how we open and close. How do we turn heartless and mindless when we feel threatened? We welcome feedback about our blind spots because we remember how dangerously unpredictable this secondary infection called "aggression" can be. It might only keep us awake for a night or two, but without warning it can take a turn and destroy our lifelines: the relationships we depend on.

When the light turns red, we shift into a me-first position and heartlessly stop caring who gets hurt. We're like a drunk swinging a sword around a crowded room. At some point we can even convince ourselves that hurting others is a good thing. It will make us feel better. This is the madness of red-light thinking.

Red-light patterns take us away from the truth of the present moment. Heartless-mind communication can be brutally blunt, using the shock waves of aggression to gain the upper hand in a situation. On the other extreme, mindless-heart communication is vague and hard to pin down. Putting these patterns under the microscope of mindfulness, we see more clearly how acting out or suppressing pain blocks compassion toward ourselves and others.

Go with the green light: Make the intention to maintain a we-first view of keeping the listener in mind when speaking.

When the light is red, stop: Set boundaries to prevent damaging other people's reputations, especially when conflict or anger arises. Watch out for all the ways we suppress empathy and turn heartless.

Be careful when the light is yellow: The core fear of the aggressive and judgmental false self is that it may be unforgivable. When we resist pain, we lose the resilience of forgiveness. So bring forgiveness and clarity—compassionate insight—to the pain of conflict and anger.

JOURNAL EXERCISE

A. *Explore replacing barriers with boundaries.*

1. Call to mind a time when you successfully kept your heart and mind open when someone else's light was

red. What were the conditions that supported you at that time?

2. What is the difference between closing down, or putting a barrier up, and being open to someone else's No Trespassing signs?

3. What does it mean to bring sympathetic understanding to your own mindless patterns?

4. How does this help you reconnect with others?

B. *Explore two structures for "telling the truth," open and closed.*

1. Open, Green-Light Self-expression:

Awake body: Describe your direct sense perceptions. Example: "When I saw you walk away . . ."

Tender heart: Put into words the primary (green-light) emotions that arose. Example: "I felt sad."

Open mind: Be curious about what this experience means to you. Example: "I wondered if you didn't want to hear what I was saying."

Action: What do you need or want to do next? Example: "So I'd like to find a better time for us to talk."

2. Closed, Red-Light Self-expression:

Perceptions: Describe the trigger event. For example, "When you walked away."

Interpretation: Describe the story line or self-talk that "edited" this event. For example, "This is hopeless."

Reaction: How did this story line make you feel?

Action: What did you do next? For example, "Depressed, angry." For example, "I resolved never to talk to you again."

FOUR STAGES OF HEARTLESSNESS

Lucas glared at the For Sale sign in front of his house. "I worked my ass off for twenty years to pay for this place, to build a happy future for me and my partner, and now she tells me she wants a divorce. She's destroyed my life." Unlike Dr. Abuelaish, most of us react to painful crises in our life by making a difficult situation worse. Often we try to cope with the feeling of powerlessness by projecting blame outward onto someone we turn into an enemy. Instead of experiencing the irritation or heartbreak directly, we get caught up in our own aggressive story lines and end up creating more harm for ourselves by burning our bridges behind us.

Lucas's outburst demonstrates how quickly pain can escalate into aggression when our communication light is red. If we listen carefully, we can identify four stages in this escalation. Each step he takes causes him to close his heart further to the woman he claims to love. Whether we're dealing with bullies on the playground, ethnic hatred in a village, or the corrosion of a marriage, these are the stages that make tenderhearted human beings cruel. In his own words, here are some further comments from Lucas that highlight these four stages of heartless mind:

1. "This shouldn't be happening to me." (complaint/criticism)
2. "She has all the power. Look what she's doing to me." (divisiveness)
3. "It's all her fault. She's out to get me." (blame)
4. "If she thinks she can get any spousal support from me after what she's done to me, she's out of her mind." (retaliation)

When we practice mindful communication, we can learn to recognize each one of these stages when they enter our conversations. By stopping at these red-light signals, we can put up firewalls to prevent aggression from spreading, not only with others but also within our own minds.

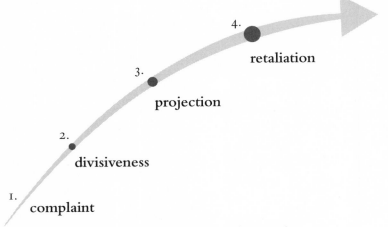

Fig. 3. Four Stages of heartless mind.

Complaint/Criticism

The first stage of heartlessness is the impulse to reject pain rather than relate to it. Sophia, who suffers from chronic physical pain, describes this clearly: "Pain has a way of bonding with fear." Instead of surrounding our pain with compassion and open-minded curiosity, fear causes us to mindlessly shut down and redirect our attention into exit strategies.

For Lucas, the pain of losing his home and his marriage was mixed with the fear that he didn't deserve to be happy and was being punished. His mind raced to catastrophic conclusions, and this was reflected in his choice of words: "destroy," "blown apart," "disaster," "impossible." To push away from his fear and pain, he's locking himself into a bunker mentality and going to war.

The belief that "this shouldn't be happening" is an example of toxic certainty, which we discussed in chapter 3. It holds out the illusion of solid ground when things are falling apart. Other ways of stating it would be "What did I do to deserve this?" or "How could she do this to me?" It isn't easy to accommodate unexpected losses and suffering in our life, but it's even more difficult when we push them away. As George, a dying hospice patient, said to me recently, "Complaining is a waste of time, and I have no more time to waste."

When we turn away from pain, we don't listen to what it is telling us. This communication shutdown makes us feel even more powerless and fearful. Complaining builds on this powerlessness by shifting the responsibility for our suffering somewhere else. It sets Lucas up to feel victimized by his wife. When he succeeds in getting his friends to agree with him, his aggression becomes more solid.

Lucas is up against the most painful crisis in his life, and what is becoming clear is that his red-light conversations are making him more miserable. With mindfulness, we don't have to wait for major events such as this. We can learn to become resilient by intercepting our reactions to smaller, everyday irritations.

My friend Peg moved to a small Mexican town about ten years ago. She made this comment:

> Over time I noticed how much happier my Mexican friends are with the ordinary ups and downs of community life. They live so much closer together and are quite accustomed to sharing living space with several generations. I'm sure they are just as irritated by one another as we are, but the difference seems to be that they don't see any point in complaining. Instead of trying to control the other person, they simply learn to become more patient.

I had a recent experience of what Peg was talking about. New neighbors moved in upstairs, above our apartment. The previous owners were a quiet, elderly couple, and I'd become accustomed to the silence in my home. Then the new family moved in like a herd of elephants. I normally think of myself as easygoing and child-friendly, but I noticed changes in my inner conversations, within the privacy of my own mind. I started mentally scanning the strata rules to see if there was a violation I could complain about.

Then I traveled to visit friends in Europe and stayed in an apartment in Rome. The sounds of children upstairs felt normal, along with the chatter of the elderly people on benches on the sidewalk outside the building. I loved this sense of feeling connected to the people around us. Simply changing the story associated with the sounds I was hearing defused the negative reaction. I switched from, "This should not be happening" to "This is happening, and that's OK."

Please remember that what we are talking about here are red-light reactions, not the healthy problem solving that needs to be done to fix a green-light situation. We'll discuss that topic in chapter 6.

THE ANTIDOTE TO COMPLAINT/CRITICISM: ACCEPTING THINGS AS THEY ARE

We live in an impermanent world—a sunny weekend turns into a rainy Monday morning; our bodies age and get sick; overnight, the price of gas shoots up. Our moods change and we feel irritated, hurt, uncomfortable. The antidote to complaint and criticism is to make peace with all these everyday communication breakdowns. Just as peacemakers connect with difficult people and situations that the rest of us hope would just disappear, we can learn to accommodate discomfort gently rather than pushing it away.

Gentleness is resilient. It gives us the power to absorb insults and blame and even say "I'm sorry" when it is really the other person who has caused the injustice. We do whatever it takes to keep the channel of communication open, and we wait patiently when it closes. We can do this without losing personal dignity or compromising the power of our own truth, because we know that the causes of war and aggression are born right in that moment when pain, or even the fear of pain, arises in our mind.

The slogan "When the light turns red, stop" is a first step in paying attention when that clenching feeling happens. It reminds us to pause and stay open when we meet life's uncomfortable moments. If we can practice holding steady at times like this, accepting what we cannot change, we're cutting the root of all the aggression in this world right where it starts.

JOURNAL EXERCISE

1. Think of an example in your life when you made a relationship to something irritating instead of struggling to push it away. Describe that experience.
2. What are the unavoidable sufferings in your life today?
3. How can you bring greater acceptance, gentleness, and compassion to these unavoidable sufferings?

Divisiveness

Lucas was fixated in a "victim stance," playing out a script that said that his wife had all the power while he had none. Having rejected our pain as something that shouldn't be happening, the second stage of heartless communication is turning the challenging person into an enemy. We do this by drawing the line between "us" and "them." Divisiveness hardens when we dehumanize the other person by using labels.

A workshop participant named Tony gave the following example:

> No matter how much I think I've made progress with my mindfulness practice, it all seems to dissolve when I'm behind the wheel. If the guy in front of me is too slow, he's a moron. If he's too fast, he's an asshole. And it

seems everyone fits into one of those two categories. Everyone but me.

A common form of divisiveness is to avoid a direct conversation with a person with whom we're in conflict by involving a third person. This is the infamous triangle configuration. One of my coworkers, Barbara, said to me, "I don't know why Robert thinks he can represent our group. He doesn't care about *my* ideas. He's incompetent and self-centered." Then there was an awkward moment when she paused for me to agree with her. I took a deep breath and asked if we could find time to talk about it later in the day.

THE ANTIDOTE TO DIVISIVENESS: BRIDGING THE DIVIDE

When Barbara and I met again later to discuss this, I began by telling her something about the mindful-communication workshops I was teaching. I explained the benefits of using a we-first approach to communication, how it was in her own best interest to keep the channel open to Robert. I invited her to use me as a sounding board so that when she talked with him, she'd speak gently, clearly distinguishing between her personal interpretations and the facts. For example, Barbara could say,

> "Robert, whenever we meet to discuss our work project, I feel as though you're not interested in my ideas. I realize this is my interpretation of the situation, but it comes up because you're in charge of the agenda and there's no time set aside for feedback during our meetings. In the future, would you please make more time for discussion."

Practicing ahead of time, Barbara was able to keep a respectful relationship with Robert and thereby increased her chances of resolving the problem. When we engage in triangulation, on the other hand, the price we pay is to create a vicious circle that makes apology and forgiveness less possible.

Another way to interrupt divisiveness is to refrain from generalizations and labels. A clue that we're putting someone in a pigeonhole is when we use the words *always* and *never.* "John is always criticizing me." "Martha never asks for help." To reverse this habit, we can practice a communication exercise called "Exceptions":

> John is always criticizing me, except for those times when he isn't.
> Mary never asks for help, except for those times when she does.

When we're divisive, we filter out details and overlook the common ground we share with other people. The antidote, then, is to reclaim this common ground. We can tune in to *tender heart,* the mixing zone that softens the divisions between "'us" and "them."

Blame

Lucas is convinced that his partner is having an affair, and this has become part of his story about why she is leaving him. What he fails to mention is that he himself has had two affairs that she's unaware of. Focusing on the harm she's done to him, on his victim stance, keeps Lucas's attention away from considering that the breakdown of the marriage had anything to do with his own behavior.

Once the divisive barrier is in place, it becomes a projection screen for all kinds of blaming story lines. It's as though the mirrorlike clarity of open mind goes into reverse and the outside world ends up reflecting back our fears instead of giving us fresh information. Everything we perceive ends up being about "me." The lawn mower in the backyard tells me I'm lazy. The phone call from my friend interrupts my peace and quiet. When the light is red, the barrier distorts everything, and we want to know, *Is this good for me or bad for me?*

Heartless story lines give us hints about the parts of ourselves we've rejected. As we've seen, the habit of shutting down to pain leaves a history of neglecting our own emotional injuries. Without compassionate insight, these injuries remain frozen, unconscious memories that manifest as projections. A prisoner I worked with named Ross is an extreme example. As a teenager, Ross was tortured by the fear that he was gay. His parents' rigid religious beliefs made it impossible for him to accept his sexual feelings. So he shut down and projected his self-hatred outward. One night his inner conflict played itself out with a tragic result. He started drinking in the late afternoon, and by nine P.M. he found himself in a local gay bar. He was on fire with intense craving for intimacy with a man. But when an attractive young man named Matt approached him, Ross froze. He blacked out and remembers nothing until waking up hours later in jail. He was charged and later convicted for savagely punching Matt, causing him permanent brain damage.

Ross's story highlights how we reject parts of ourselves that we fear by projecting them onto others. To create a culture of peace in our homes, workplaces, and communities, we need to open up a dialogue with all these unforgivable, unlovable parts of ourselves that we're afraid of. We get acquainted with them when we take a fresh look at the people in our lives who push our buttons. Our "Can't Trust" button might come up around certain authority figures. Our "Lazy Bum" button might be pushed by people who move at a different pace than our own. There are those people we agree with, and we like to have them around, and then there are the ones who make us feel uncomfortable because they are so different. Practicing mindful communication is a way to make room on our path to learn something from every conversation that occurs in our life, pleasant or unpleasant.

When the light is red, we give away our power by finding fault in others. Closed conversations are like Ponzi schemes. We try to win our friends over to our side, to believe our story but not investigate the facts too closely. At its root, blaming depends on the seesaw of "either-or" thinking: "Either Josh is bad and I'm good, or, if he's OK, it must be me who is bad." When you strip away the elaborate story lines and justifications, red-light thinking is crude, because it depends on this primitive dualistic view.

THE ANTIDOTE TO PROJECTING BLAME: DISSOLVING DUALISTIC BARRIERS

Understanding how the dualistic mind works helps dissolve this rigid "good/bad" barrier. Dualism creates all kinds of reference points that depend on each other, such as good/bad, short/tall, pleasant/unpleasant. These reference points are helpful ways of navigating our everyday life, but they are always only relative. One way we can move past them in our conversations is by mixing them up. We can try adding a negative quality to an object of craving ("Remember how sick you will feel tomorrow if you binge tonight") or a positive quality to a negative object ("She's not all-bad").

Another strategy could be that when blame arises in a conversation, we might reclaim some of the negative features as our own. Here's an example:

Sally: "I can't stand Joe. He's such a jerk, the way he undermines me at our weekly meetings, interrupting my presentation as if my work isn't as important as his."

Bella: "I can sympathize with how you feel, but I see myself doing the same thing as Joe all the time. I, too, get excited about what I'm saying and interrupt other people."

By taking on some of the negative features that Sally is projecting onto Joe, Bella is dissolving the barrier and helping her friend feel a bit more compassion, not only toward Joe but also toward herself.

Another way to intervene during a blaming conversation is to use reflective listening to mirror back the facts without coloring them with our personal evaluation. "Joe is sitting back on his chair with his feet on the desk" is a description, a fact, whereas "Joe is lazy" is a judgment.

Retaliation

> This is certain, that a man that studieth revenge keeps his wounds green, which otherwise would heal and do well.
>
> —SIR FRANCIS BACON

By the time Lucas met with his lawyer, conversations between him and his friends had escalated his rage to such a degree that he wasn't even interested in a collaborative process. Being convinced his wife was out to get him, he hired an aggressive attorney and tried to win full custody of the children by proving she was an unfit mother. When the family-court judge heard the case, he threw it out. Ironically, the court fees and lawyer bills ate up any profit he would have made from selling his home.

Aggression is most destructive when we give ourselves permission to punish someone else for the pain we feel. Retaliative story lines tell us that hurting the other person or group will give us relief. For instance, when someone cuts in front of us on the freeway, we say, "I can't let him get away with this."

When communication is closed, things tend to go badly. We ignore the domino effect that our words trigger. If we look closely, we may notice that our intention isn't to communicate at all, but rather to punish our listener. This is a sure sign that we've turned the other person into an object.

Mark and Maria were adjusting to the first sleepless year as parents of a baby who had frequent bouts of colic. Mark was feeling frustrated and resentful about the loss of intimacy in their marriage. One evening they got a babysitter so that they could have some quality time together. But Mark wasn't in the mood to have a good time. He wanted Maria to feel jealous, to punish her for repeatedly saying no when he wanted to make love over the past month. So he tricked her by saying how important it was to be honest with each other, and then he proceeded to tell her all the details of the intimate conversation he had had with his attractive new colleague during a recent business trip. This scheme backfired; Maria walked out of the restaurant and took a taxi home.

Later, in a counseling session, Mark started to understand how he had convinced himself that hurting Maria was the right thing to do. Like a spin doctor, justification uses all kinds of mental tricks to support our red-light self-deception. One trick is to reverse the meaning of certain words. For instance, at first Mark said that he wanted me to "validate" his point of view, but when he used the word *validate,* he actually meant *justify.* He wanted me to go along with his story, which is exactly what red-light conversations do. However, justification is the exact opposite of validation, which means giving a reality check. When we insist that other people support our projections, rather than telling us the truth, this is a red flag. We're covering up the obvious, conning ourselves into thinking that what is harmful is actually good for us. Justification is like slick advertising that persuades us to eat junk food as if it were healthy and to reject nourishing food because it's inconvenient to prepare.

When Mark was finally able to let go of his justifications, he realized that he genuinely wanted to be honest with Maria but simply didn't know how. It took a lot of courage to push past his comfort zone to finally tell Maria the truth: that he was feeling jealous and hurt that all her attention was going to the baby. He admitted that he'd wanted to hurt her by punishing her but also to elicit a sign of her loyalty to him by trying to get her to feel jealous. He felt awkward sharing these vulnerable feelings with her, but once he started to talk about them, he felt like he was reconnecting with a deeper truth within himself. At this point he saw how harmful his retaliation scheme had been by contrast.

Rather than trying to cover it up or act it out, Mark used mindfulness practice to simply stay present with the pain of his longing to reconnect with Maria. To do this, he practiced mindful presence: being silent, bringing his attention to his breath, to the sensations in his body, letting his thoughts come and go in a relaxed way. Gradually his body, heart, and mind began communicating with each other. He felt his emotions as sensations and energy in his body, and only then did his genuine words start to appear. The word *frustration* changed to *fear,* and then into *sadness.* Before communicating with Maria, he needed to learn how to comfort himself when he felt these feelings, to be gentle and accommodating and honest about how he could meet his own needs so that he could then be more available to her and the baby.

After a time apart, Mark and Maria made a fresh start. He apologized to her with such authenticity that the barrier between them started to dissolve. Maria reached over and took his hand. In spite of the crisis, or perhaps because of it, a new level of trust had entered their relationship.

It wasn't easy for Mark to expose his vulnerable feelings, because he judged them as irrational and immature. But telling his emotional truth to Maria was a risk worth taking. He did this in three steps: First, by reclaiming the problem as his own, not hers; second, by sincerely apologizing for the harm he had done; and finally, by making the decision to care for his own emotional needs instead of asking Maria to do this for him.

Here's a summary of the self-reflection log from Mark's homework journal:

Red–light pattern:

Body: When I see you holding the baby,
Interpretation: I think you don't love me anymore.
Red-light emotion: I get angry and want revenge.
Justification: I tell myself that I have the right to equal time.

Green–light pattern:

Awake body: When I see you holding the baby,
Tender heart: I feel longing and sadness.
Open mind: I'm curious about the changes in our relation-
ship and afraid of where they may lead.

THE ANTIDOTE TO RETALIATION: FORGIVENESS AND RECONCILIATION

> Peace is not only the absence of conflict, but also requires a
> positive, dynamic participatory process where dialogue is en-
> couraged and conflicts are solved in a spirit of mutual under-
> standing and cooperation.
> —DECLARATION AND PROGRAMME OF ACTION ON A
> CULTURE OF PEACE (UN GENERAL ASSEMBLY
> RESOLUTION A/53/243, 1999)

A powerful antidote to retaliation is to develop a forgiving nature. If we're ready to unmask, asking the question, What
would it take to simply forgive? can clarify our hidden agendas.
Like our friend Paul, for various reasons many of us overreact
to our human failings and conclude that mistakes make us unacceptable, unforgivable, and basically bad. Bringing compassion to our inner "good/bad" scripts allows us to have a
forgiving view of other people's limitations.

When we heal the part of ourselves that feels unforgivable,
we're able to absorb a little injustice now and then for the

benefit of greater peace. Learning how to return to the present moment with mindfulness is like a safety net when we're triggered by anger or hatred.

When Archbishop Desmond Tutu spoke in support of restorative justice as a means of healing the South African community after Apartheid, he emphasized the point that forgiveness is not to condone or minimize the awfulness of an atrocity or wrong. It is to recognize the wrongness while at the same time choosing a we-first stance, which is to acknowledge the essential humanity of the perpetrator and to give that perpetrator the possibility of making a new beginning. Tutu went on to say that forgiveness is a way of acknowledging the essential goodness of people and to have faith in their potential to change.

Having worked in a maximum security prison program with sex offenders, including men like Norman, I have personal experience of the truth of Tutu's approach. Forgiveness is not about punitive justice, which depends on the view of retaliation, but it is an essential component of restorative justice, justice that aims to restore the social balance that the wrongdoing has disturbed.

To see how forgiveness fits into the practice of mindful communication, let's look at three important points:

1. Forgiveness is not the same thing as a mindless-heart pattern of ignoring harm that's been done and suppressing our truth.

2. Forgiveness is about trust. To be genuine, it needs to come from a vision of "we-first"—recognizing our interdependence with others.

3. Forgiveness comes from a deep longing to restore a sense of balance and wholeness to our relationships and our community.

SILENCING OURSELVES

The four stages of heartlessness can also be directed inward. In this reverse pattern, we turn blame and punishment onto ourselves rather than letting it out. Let's take a closer look at this red-light signal, which is what I call "minimizing." Here's an example.

While we were visiting recently, my friend Sarah was sitting across the table, pouring a cup of tea. She accidentally tipped over the teapot, spilling hot tea all over her hand. At that moment I cried out, almost as though her hand were my own. I felt overcome by a tenderhearted concern for her, and my priority was to attend to her burn. But Sarah did not cry out, nor did she make any effort to take care of her hand. She brushed my compassionate response aside. I watched her jaw tighten while she jumped up and vigorously cleaned up the spilled tea on the table, berating herself all the while. It was confusing and painful to see my friend treat herself so harshly.

Sarah denied the truth of her reality and silenced that part of herself that needed help. I knew some things about Sarah's past. As a child, she had worked in the family restaurant with her father. He was a single parent who drank too much and mistreated her. Sarah had adapted to the dangerous relationship with her father by training herself to suppress her body's natural responses and her needs. What I witnessed during the tea incident was how Sarah had learned to switch off the distress signal from her burned hand. She was automatically replaying the pattern that she'd been so well trained in. Her internalized father's voice told her that no matter what she feels, she has no right to ask for help—her duty to clean up is more important than the pain in her hand. When Sarah suppressed her cry for help, an internal bully dominated her, just as her alcoholic father had. Sarah's burned hand didn't take long to heal, but her red-light patterns will intensify each time she replays them, causing her more and more suffering.

As we gain experience in practicing mindful communication, it's possible to notice how all three lights can flash during a single conversation. Noticing ourselves shift from open to fearful and then to closed communication enables us to recognize this process in someone else. Understanding what it feels like to minimize our needs and suppress the messages from our body and emotions makes it easier to respectfully stop when someone else's light turns red, rather than push forward and try to force the situation. At the same time, we can both stop and remain open. With Sarah, at some point I realized that she was sending me a signal that told me to stop. Being mindfully present with a friend when communication shuts down is like stepping into the role of a loving parent with a child who's having a nightmare.

If someone we're communicating with suddenly shuts down, we need to be flexible enough to abandon our hope for two-way communication. We can shift into the one-way street of mindful presence. Like shock absorbers on a bumpy road, mindfulness gives us emotional stability and resiliency. Holding steady and feeling the sadness of being cut off from our friend when she is in pain is a lonely experience, in contrast to minimizing and denying that pain.

SILENCING OTHERS

As we've seen, refraining from aggressive communication isn't the same thing as putting a lid on ourselves, suppressing parts of ourselves that we think of as unacceptable. Mindfulness shows us how painful and unnecessary aggression is. When we refrain from harsh speech and gossip, we begin to notice more subtle forms of aggression, such as how we silence people when they say what we don't want to hear.

Silencing is like a stealth weapon in our blame arsenal. This form of aggression often goes unnoticed. We silence other people whenever we edit out information that makes us feel uncomfortable. I've seen myself do this time and time again in my communication. Here's an example. My son, Sheehan, is one of my teachers when it comes to compassion. When he was about six years old, we were living in a small mountain cabin while I was participating in a group retreat. It was midwinter and bitterly cold. We were walking through a snowy meadow when he spotted one of the nearly wild cattle that wandered around the land. "Look how cold he is!" he said urgently.

"Honey, he has that big warm fur coat to keep him warm," I stupidly replied.

"No, look, look! Look into his eyes," he insisted.

If this had been an ordinary day and we were driving to the supermarket, I would have continued to ignore my son's sensitivity, silencing him in a patronizing way. But fortunately, I was in a retreat, and there were no other distractions as we trudged through the snow toward our cabin. So I took another look.

There was a crust of snow on the steer's forehead, and he was standing stiffly, bracing himself against the cold wind. This poor animal was clearly suffering, in spite of his winter coat. Suddenly, like my child, I was overwhelmed with sadness and powerlessness. These were the very feelings that my glib story was trying to suppress. If the doorway to our cabin had been bigger, that animal would probably have spent the night with us. Instead, Sheehan and I stayed up late, in the glow of the woodstove, imagining new kinds of human dwellings that would always have room for animals who needed shelter. When we're powerless to do anything in reality, we can at least make the wish that they might find some relief.

STOPPING WHEN THE LIGHT IS RED

The practice of gentle speech tempers our reactions by meeting our uncomfortable, irritating, or painful experiences with compassion, insight, and attention, the three components of our natural communication system. To do this, we turn our attention inward and change our relationship to pain. This includes not only the original discomfort we are trying to block but also the suffering created by our red-light patterns. To do this, we apply the slogan "When the light turns red, stop" to interrupt the chain reactions that steal our attention away.

To interrupt the red light, we need the following four skills:

- To *distinguish* red from green and see the difference between our primary, green-light pain and the secondary, red-light aggression
- To *recognize* our own red-light signals
- To *interrupt,* or disengage from, the momentum of the aggressive current
- To *soften* by turning our attention to the original pain that we've been avoiding

Altogether, these four skills can transform aggression into compassion. The best way to develop these skills is within a green zone, or retreat. As we previously discussed, a green zone is a space for meaningful dialogue either alone, using meditation or contemplative practices, or with other people who are practicing mindful communication. In the previous chapter we saw how mindful listening brings encouragement and healing to that part of ourselves that we judge as bad.

Stopping at the red light gives us a chance to create this kind of compassionate listening space for ourselves. Whether alone or with a friend, we need space to deeply listen to our pain and fear. During an argument, when we feel the urge to go for a walk, we're following a healthy instinct to back away before we say or do something to harm our relationship. But without a method for working with our mind, it's quite possible we'll return from a time-out with more emotional weapons than we left with. With mindfulness we can transform a time-out into a "time-in," a green-zone retreat. A green zone gives us the emotional safety to turn inward and listen to ourselves. It's time to arouse compassionate insight for the sadness, powerlessness, and pain of feeling disconnected.

If we can find the support to stay open even for just a few minutes, it's possible to notice that the crisis reaction has a beginning and an end. Riding this energy is like holding the wheel steady when we unexpectedly drive into a dark tunnel. The more we become familiar with our reactions to uncertainty, the less power they have to throw us off course.

Let's look more closely at these four skills and talk about how we can train in them, both alone and with the help of a green-zone friend, someone who is also practicing these principles of mindful communication.

The First Skill: Being Willing to Look at Our Own Patterns to Distinguish Red from Green

A courageous first step for dissolving barriers is simply being willing to look more closely at our patterns, the chain reactions that turn our original pain into a secondary layer of aggression. To do this, we use a practice called *self-reflection*. Because it's difficult to notice red-light patterns while they're in full force, we choose a situation that happened recently and analyze it.

Self-reflection can be done in a variety of ways:

- As a contemplative meditation
- By writing in a freestyle manner in a journal or using an analysis like the journal exercise below.
- By making a collage or another art form, as demonstrated by Olivia's "photo album," which is discussed at length in the next chapter
- In a contemplative dialogue with a friend who knows how to listen mindfully

The practice of self-reflection takes advantage of an interesting feature of the mind—the fact that imaginary or remembered stories can arouse emotions just as if they were happening in real-life present time. This is why our secondary emotions torture us for nights on end as we replay painful scenarios over and over again in our mind. But now, practicing self-reflection, we can engage with this process mindfully.

We begin self-reflection with a few minutes of silent meditation. Come back to the body, the rhythm of our breath, gently letting go of thoughts when they distract us. Now, we think back to a specific situation when communication closed down or turned aggressive. Notice how we start to relive the experience in the present moment. This is helpful because, like a scientist in a lab, we're bringing our reactions out of the fear-based situation and examining them under ideal conditions, lessening the sense of urgency that normally contributes to mindlessness.

My teacher, Sakyong Mipham Rinpoche, compares the view of "me-first" to looking through the wrong end of binoculars—the happiness we're looking for becomes ever more distant. This is an uncomfortable realization, but it can be a breakthrough in our practice of mindful communication. Once we see this, we're one step closer to turning the binoculars around and taking a closer look at what we're doing.

Like an inquisitive journalist, we ask ourselves questions to understand more about what exactly happened with our communication when we shut down. Sitting here in the relative safety of home, I flash back to one of my experiences reacting to Robert. In my mind, I see him walking down the hall. This is the trigger event. Now the movie begins. Right here in the present moment I start to feel certain sensations. I notice tension arising in my body. Where is this tension? What color is it? What shape is it? What part of my body is it gripping?

I notice a defensive script forming in my mind. What is this story line? Who are the cast of characters? What is the last act of the play? I notice my heart tighten and contract as the story plays out. I don't want to look vulnerable. I feel like a medieval knight holding up a shield. My perception shrinks—the world no longer feels like a safe or wonderful place. I feel like I'm looking through a peephole in my helmet, preoccupied with my personal security. Life becomes about him on one side and me on the other.

Analyzing even one reactive pattern helps us understand

how we cut ourselves off from friendliness when we shut down. When the light is red, people and situations, indeed everything "out there," is screened through self-protective questions: *Will this hurt me? Do I need this? Should I ignore this?*

Then we go on to analyze what happened next. What kind of mask did I put on? How did things develop after that? False confidence, aggression, and other tactics of the red light do not bring us security. Such tactics are defective. They take us farther away from the emotional safety we're seeking in our relationships.

JOURNAL EXERCISE

1. Choose an incident when you noticed your communication shutting down. What exactly was the trigger event?
2. Here and now, what sensations or tensions arise in your body? Where is this tension?
3. What is the defensive script in your mind? What is the story line? Who are the cast of characters? What is the last act of the play?
4. Do you notice your heart tightening and contracting? How dangerous is it to look vulnerable?
5. What did you say or do in this situation?
6. What would a we-first response in this situation require? Imagine what that might look like in realistic detail.

The process of reflecting on our communication patterns allows little flashes of green light, positive interruptions of curiosity and sadness. We begin to realize that our aggressive patterns of speech spill out into the world from inner-bully voices within our own mind. Seeing this, compassionate insight begins to dawn.

An internal green zone is created by maintaining a daily

contemplative practice that combines meditation with self-reflection. This gives us a way of processing and gaining insight into the unspoken conversations within our own mind. An external green zone is formed by having a circle of friends who deeply listen to us when we feel overwhelmed by aggression, anxiety, craving, or jealousy. Like my friend Ann, they can help us open to the original pain or sadness we're blocking.

A green-zone conversation is like a social form of meditation. Our friend helps us come back to the freshness of the present moment by helping us distinguish red-light reactions from green. Our green-zone friend reminds us that aggressive speech has no value. It doesn't give us power. Heartless communication makes painful situations worse instead of better.

Stopping at the red light is essentially a choice to favor reality over our inner fictions. When intense reactions are taking hold of us, taking a break from the situation gives us a chance to return to the present moment. We don't have to go it alone. This is a good time to ask a green-zone friend, someone like Ann, for support and feedback. A green-zone friend is someone who also practices mindfulness meditation and who can lend us some clarity and kindness so that we can separate our imaginary fictions from the facts of the present moment.

My meditation teacher tells the story of a man who went out in his backyard in the early morning, before dawn, and spotted a coiled object in the grass. In the dim light he was sure it was a poisonous snake. His heart was pounding with fear. He was totally preoccupied by all the different ways he could get rid of it. A half hour later the sun rose and he took another look outside. Seeing more clearly, he realized that the snake he was so afraid of was merely a garden hose.

When we exaggerate, we're like the man who sees a hose as a snake. Another version of the story can describe how we minimize, silencing our own truth. This often happens with mindless-heart reactions that overrule common sense because of our emotional needs. Minimizing is like seeing a poisonous snake as nothing more than a garden hose. The snake could represent an abusive partner, or a line of cocaine, or any of the everyday toxins we allow into our lives. When we're blinded by emotional hunger, we can be persuaded to ignore poisonous snakes and start thinking of them as helpful.

A green-zone friend might say to us, "I know that you're really upset right now and you're convinced that you need to go out and beat up that object in the backyard, but please trust me, it's only a garden hose."

It is important to remember that red-light emotions are created by thoughts. This is what distinguishes them from green-light emotions, which relate directly to reality. Mindfulness meditation trains us to wake up and return to the present moment when we're hooked by a fictional story in our mind. Toxic emotional reactions such as aggression, addiction, and envy originate from not trusting ourselves. Until we can listen properly to our own body, heart, and mind, we're unable to hear the messages that tell us what we really need.

JOURNAL EXERCISE

How do you discern the difference between your personal projections and the truth of the situation? Come up with your own examples of seeing a garden hose as a snake, or conversely, seeing a poisonous snake as a garden hose.

Recognizing Our Own Red-Light Signals

A green-zone friend can also help us with recognizing our own red-light signals, which are normally hidden in our blind spot. Learning to tell the truth about our own aggressive patterns isn't easy. It seems the more honest we are with ourselves, the more self-deception we uncover. It starts to feel like we're always either exaggerating or suppressing information. Because mindfulness practice makes us see this more clearly, we might wonder if our training is making things worse instead of better. So it's important to encourage ourselves with gentle humor and sympathy for our situation, realizing we're not alone. Everyone on the planet has his or her own version of these unseen forces that resist openness. We need to accept our own limitations with a friendly attitude.

Mindfulness teachers often compare the natural synchronicity of body, heart, and mind to a well-trained horse and rider. But we also need to remember that our starting point is the opposite of this: our habit of mindless communication is like a rider with no reins; it feels like unseen forces are riding us instead of the other way around. To playfully encourage my students to recognize their aggressive patterns, I introduce them to a few challenging "lesson ponies" I met in my childhood.

I took riding lessons from a talented but impoverished dressage teacher named Mrs. Marshall. After immigrating to Canada from England, she bought a small piece of land with a decrepit barn and put together a stable of lesson ponies, a bunch of misfits that she'd rescued from various dead-end situations. My first lesson was on Tarnish, a faded brown mare that Mrs. Marshall saved from the dog-food factory. Tarnish had a cranky disposition and was famous for simply stopping dead in her tracks whenever she wanted to. Nothing that a child could do would get her to move until she was ready.

Weeks later, I moved on to ride Tinker, a little roan gelding with a devilish glint in his eye. He had the kind of criminal personality that would trick you into a cooperative relationship and then, when he'd won your trust, out of the blue his ears would go flat back and he'd bare his teeth and go after one of the other horses like a Mafia hit man.

When I got a bit older, I rode Twig, a huge chestnut with a stubbly mane who looked like the legendary Trojan horse. He had a blunt temperament and would just slog along without giving much thought to what was in front of him. Twig was a recovered draft horse, and like an armored tank, he'd sometimes plow right through our homemade fence and out onto the street.

The most memorable of these early riding lessons were the ones marked by sheer terror on the back of Elvie O'Maxie. She was a retired Standardbred trotter that Mrs. Marshall rescued after she'd worked twelve years at the racetrack. Elvie was a gentle soul, but she was prone to reliving her past, flashing back to the starting gate and then taking off around the track at full tilt, with me clinging on for dear life to her mane. Being out of control like this, with no idea what disastrous ending was in store for me, was a rite of passage that repeated itself countless times in the years before I finally learned how to make a relationship with a horse.

Eventually, mindfulness training can stabilize our mind so that we gain the power to pick up the reins and align our speech with our intentions. But the starting point is to make friends with the lesson pony we're riding right now. What are the unseen inner forces that cause us to react aggressively in ways we don't intend?

Bringing gentle honesty and humor to our own difficult lesson ponies is the key to being more patient with other people who have similarly challenging communication styles. Each of us has our own unique version of the red light and our personal story about how it originated. But the result is the same: the desynchronization of our natural communication system—our thoughts are saying one thing, our body is expressing something else, and we have no idea what our heart is telling us. Being compartmentalized and off balance is so familiar that we lose sight of what is true. We're chronically operating on misinformation, so it's understandable that we confuse the idea of "open communication" with "anything goes."

Minimizing, justifying, ignoring, and *exaggerating* are four red-light signals that we can explore using the horses as examples.

MINIMIZING: TARNISH, THE PONY WHO DIGS IN HER HEELS

The first red-light signal to watch out for is the communication barrier itself. The flow of conversation hits a snag and we start editing information by either overreacting or underreacting to an event in the present moment. In our meditation practice, we train to notice this shift because it happens when we become distracted from paying attention to our breathing and instead get lost in our thoughts. When these thoughts and inner stories overrule the information coming to us in the present moment, our communication light goes from green to red.

When Sarah wanted to understand her own red-light signals, I told her the story of the lesson ponies. She identified with Tarnish, the pony who would stop and shut down for no apparent reason. Rather than exaggerating her reactions, her inner editor minimized them. When she was in pain, she shut down and directed her aggression inward.

By identifying with Tarnish, Sarah was able to feel compassion for this old mare who had painful stiff joints from years of service. Since Sarah loved animals, it wasn't hard for her to feel loving-kindness for this imaginary horse. This became a bridge for her to begin to be more sympathetic with that overburdened part of herself that had no language other then to shut down.

JUSTIFYING: TINKER, THE PONY WITH A HIDDEN AGENDA

The second red-light signal to be on the lookout for is justification. Once our communication barrier is up, the inner editor in our mind takes over and our stories start spinning. These justifications are how we give ourselves permission to say or do something harmful. They create what my teacher calls "negative negativity," an additional layer of self-deception that camouflages our original painful reaction. When the communication light is red, our conversations with other people echo our inner justifications, which seem more convincing when we persuade others to agree with us.

Mark gained insight into his justifications when he heard the story of the little roan pony named Tinker. By identifying with the pony who had a hidden intention, he was able to gently understand how his justification worked in two directions, tricking not only Maria but himself as well. By the time he made a lunge and attacked Maria, he was completely convinced that this was the right thing for him to do. But his script was abruptly interrupted when she said no and marched out of the restaurant.

By paying attention to his justification, Mark practiced the mindful-communication technique of positive interruptions, staying on the lookout for any occasion when "being wrong is right." He told me with a smile that Maria was always ready to give him a hand with this, literally. Whenever he'd go off track, she'd silently hold up her hand to signal "Stop."

IGNORING: TWIG, THE BULLDOZER PONY

The third red-light signal to watch out for is ignoring, or rejecting feedback. When our communication barrier is up, our inner stories are more important than the present moment. We're not interested in reality-checking our opinions for accuracy. This is how we end up surrounding ourselves with people who can't tell us the truth. We silence people who are open and only listen to voices that agree with us. We discount people who are genuinely interested in our well-being and limit our circle to those who are in the same trap as we are.

This is what happened to Lucas. His blunt interpretation of the circumstances surrounding his divorce made no room for alternative narratives. He was a victim, and his wife was the bad guy. Anyone who thought differently was on the wrong side.

When our barrier is up like this, we become stupid and narrow-minded, like the lesson pony Twig, who could walk right through a fence. Closing the door to honest feedback from our friends is like cutting the string on a kite. Our mind drifts farther from the ground of reality and we're tossed around by the winds of imaginary fears. Our thoughts turn over and over again, further spinning our justifying scenarios. It's a common belief that we don't cause any harm with our thoughts, but this isn't true. When our mind is closed, our thoughts repeat imagined experiences that build emotional reactions. The more Lucas told his story, the more true it became. Because he was closed to feedback, Lucas blocked the path to the one thing he wanted, a happy future with his wife.

EXAGGERATING: ELVIE O'MAXIE, THE WILD PONY

In their first couples' counseling session, Eve and Sam were introducing themselves to me. I knew little about them, except that they'd been married eight years, with no children. Eve opened by saying she welcomed the opportunity to finally be honest with Sam. Then she started to escalate, venting her rage against him as if he were her most despicable enemy. "I'll tell you the truth—I hate you. I've never loved you, I was just charmed by your money. When you touch me, I feel disgusted. That's why I needed another lover. You could never make me feel the way he does—" I held up my hand to interrupt her because this kind of "honesty" was actually a verbal attack, not communication. Eve then turned her anger toward me, saying that she expected that I, as another woman, should validate her.

Eve was convinced that any emotion she felt or any story line running through her mind was "the truth." It is hard to discern the difference between green-light and red-light experiences without meditation practice. The phrase "letting down our fences," which refers to openness, doesn't mean we get rid of our relationship boundaries. Openness isn't a free-for-all, a license to dump all our emotional toxic waste onto someone else.

Like being carried away by Elvie O'Maxie, Eve's communication expressed an uncontrolled mind. Without our experiencing some mindfulness training, thoughts and emotions can take us all over the place and wreak havoc with our relationships. I subsequently met with Eve and Sam separately to help each of them clarify what they were trying to communicate to each other. It wasn't easy for Eve to let go of her rage toward Sam. I guided her in a mindfulness practice that brought her attention home, to her original body, heart, and curiosity. As she regained her balance, Eve's truth became clearer. Like Mark, she wanted to punish Sam for letting her down, for not being there when she needed him. But unlike Mark and Maria, the relationship between Sam and Eve had gone past the point of no return. Both of them knew this, but neither of them could admit to themselves that their partnership was over. They had replaced the passion of love with the passion of hatred, enacting a mindless ritual, with Sam distancing into cool detachment while Eve hotly raged against him. Practicing mindful communication was at least a way for each of them to restore personal integrity. For Sam this meant opening his heart, allowing himself to feel sadness and regret about saying goodbye. For Eve this meant accepting the truth of the ending of the relationship without blaming either herself or Sam. Thanks to their individual efforts, this couple was able to part ways with gentle dignity.

JOURNAL EXERCISE: MY STABLE OF LESSON PONIES

Give some examples of your own lesson ponies, or use mine as a starting point. How do the habits of mindlessness show up in your meditation practice? How do these patterns also manifest in your conversations with other people? For example:

- Tarnish: Out of nowhere, I suddenly shut down for no reason or cling to opinions I know are irrational.
- Tinker: I have a mean streak and want to insult or get even with someone.
- Twig: I have strong opinions and ignore other people when I'm talking.
- Elvie: Sometimes I let my anger take off without knowing where I'm going.

Interrupting the Momentum of the Aggressive Current

The third skill we need to transform aggressive speech is to interrupt the story lines that arise in our conversations to support our closed communication patterns. We can enlist the help of a trusted friend to give us feedback when our conversations turn negative. Closed communication patterns harm our relationships when we buy into them and act them out. But they have something to teach us if we can understand these patterns instead of pushing them away. Once we recognize them, we can use them as reminders to practice stopping at the red light, interrupting mindless conversations by returning to the present moment.

An image that many people have found helpful is to imagine our red-light pattern as if it were a good friend who is drunk. If we really care about this friend, we'll take away the car keys. We muster the courage to do this out of love, not out of hatred. To cut through our justifications, we have to be clear that the word *stop* really means to stop, that is, to refrain from saying anything that causes harm, either to ourselves or to others. We turn the car keys over to the part of ourselves that remembers our "we-first" commitment, which is to protect other people's reputations, even during those episodes when they seem like they are our worst enemies.

The red-light symbol is a helpful reminder that we're in

danger when our barriers are up. Going forward will put us on a collision course that only makes things worse. It moves us away from relating directly to our pain and sadness. This is the point when we benefit from having done our homework. Analyzing our red-light reactions ahead of time gives us a good idea where our reactions take us, like a drunken driver envisioning going to jail or causing a fatality.

There are two ways that a listener can positively interrupt a heartless communication pattern. The first is to literally interrupt, to bring the speaker back to the present moment, the wakefulness of body, heart, or mind.

> Julie was upset after a meeting with her divorce attorney so I asked if she'd like to step out of my office and go for a walk. It was a beautiful spring day but she was totally absorbed in re-living the painful conflict with her husband, Lucas. She was going over the story again and again. Each time her fear and anger got more intense. I felt helpless to support her, but I realized that our conversation was like one of those horses wearing blinkers, because we were in the past, not right now. So I interrupted her, asked if we could just sit down on a park bench and breathe in the beauty around us. We chose a bench that looked out on a garden full of daffodils with blossoming azalea bushes around them. The longer we looked, the more stunning they were. It took a few minutes, but finally she sighed with relief and thanked me.

A sigh of relief brings us back to the present moment, a short flash of the green light. Whenever we reconnect like this, even briefly, it is like recharging our energy, going back to the limitless source of wakefulness within us.

The second way that a listener can positively interrupt a red-light pattern is to simply mirror back what we're hearing. When the communication channel is closed, our options are limited, because two-way traffic has stopped. But we can still hold up a Stop sign by mirroring back what we've heard without any input of our own:

> Ed: "I can't stand those lazy bums who just sit around all day collecting welfare while the rest of us have to work to support them."
> Dwayne: "I understand that you believe people who are unemployed are lazy and a burden."

In this situation, Ed's red-light signal is flashing, indicating that he's not interested in feedback or another point of view. Dwayne can simply remain silent or, as in this example, he can clarify that Ed's statement is a personal opinion rather than a fact about unemployed people.

When communication is closed, speaking gently can help us meet the challenge of aggression with patience and emotional maturity. To do this, we simply hold steady and reflect back what we're hearing or seeing, like hitting the playback button on a recorder. If we can remain open, without caving in to the pressure to buy into our friend's story lines, reflective listening can make the departure point between fiction and fact more obvious. The escalating effect of aggressive speech can be interrupted with the simple gift of recognition, allowing our friend to feel respected even if we disagree with what he or she is saying.

Reflective listening interrupts justification with validation, offering a reality check to our friend. The statement "I understand that you believe this is true" shifts our focus away from the external situation and redirects our attention to the belief system that is framing it. On rare occasions, simply listening like this and reframing the discussion can pacify misunderstandings between people. A remarkable number of conflicts are easily resolved just by articulating the problem more clearly.

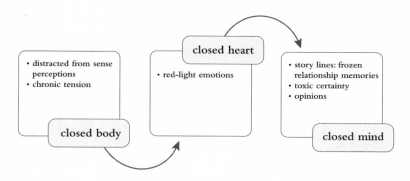

Fig. 4. Closed communication patterns.

Softening by Attending to the Original Pain

The fourth skill we need is to bring compassionate insight to the sadness and powerlessness we feel. We return to the original raw wound of our experience—an example would be Dr. Abuelaish's grief at the death of his daughters. If we were to try to block the rawness of this wound, we would infect it with hatred and aggression. However, it's possible, instead, to speak gently, with a "we-first" intention, even when we're angry. The key to doing this is to not get hooked by blame. We do need to express ourselves, but at the same time we also need to keep a protective firewall around our reactions. In order for us to be able to do this at such a challenging time, we need to apply the antidote to heartless-mind communication, which is compassionate insight.

We listen for these tender emotions by coming back to our body. The power of mindfulness brings us home to the heart we were born with. Along the way we uncover the tricks we've used to suppress or act out our pain—the ways we've tried to avoid experiencing our heart directly. The rhythm of the breath is one way our heart speaks to us. The way we listen is by allowing the breath to rise and fall at its own pace. It takes courage to relax and accept ourselves as we are. Our breath links our body, heart, and mind, and at the same time it connects our inner being with the external world. Being with our breath makes room for the pain, fear, sadness, and all the other emotions we normally try to avoid.

Simply stay present with your breath. Staying with the breath as it makes its cycle in and out of the body, as it gently disperses into the space around us, puts us back in touch with the unspoken language of our bioenergetic experience. Not judging or suppressing our emotional reactions, but instead coming back to the breath gives us a bit of distance from thoughts, making the subtle energies of tender heart easier to notice.

Once we manage to prevent our own red-light reactions, we need to hold steady with the tender yellow- and green-light emotions, the sadness of feeling cut off and misunderstood. The sadness of witnessing the suffering of others is a healthy kind of pain, an example of green-light emotion. If we can turn this sadness into the intention to see more clearly, we can use it to further motivate ourselves to practice mindfulness in our communication. In conversations, notice how we silence other people by tuning them out when they're saying things we don't want to hear. In the example given earlier in the chapter, I blocked my heart to the steer's suffering by overruling what my child was saying.

Our external conversations show us what's going on inside our mind and heart. When my son first tried to show me that the steer was suffering, I reacted to him in the same way I react to my own tender feelings, suppressing them with a preconceived idea—"Everything's fine and here's why. . . ." My heartless-mind pattern cut me off from the power of clarity. Martin Buber would say that my conversation with my son had gone from an I/Thou relationship into I/it. I'd turned my child into an object.

Practicing mindfulness opens us to sadness because, at some level, our heart grieves whenever we turn someone from "thou" to "it." Like the grief that comes with death, we feel the pain of loss when we close the door on someone, shutting our eyes and ears to who they are and refusing to hear what they are trying to tell us. So it takes a lot of courage and kindness to un-silence our pain and sadness by clearly seeing the futility of these mindless communication habits.

Gentleness reconnects us with the strength of our natural heart by opening us up to the sadness of feeling powerless when we reach our limits. When we stop running away from this sadness and embrace it fully, we then reset our intention. Instead of reacting to this sadness by shutting down, we make a promise to do whatever it takes to make a difference someday. This is the power of making an aspiration, which is a positive kind of wishful thinking.

Talking to ourselves when the communication channel has shut down is one way of putting this aspiration into practice. For example:

- May Sarah be happy. May she know that she's loved and that it's OK for her to have needs. May she be surrounded by warm and loving mother-energy so that she can heal. May all the people who are hurt and fearful, like Sarah, be relieved of their pain. May they all know love.
- May Lucas and all the people in the world who are angry at this moment be relieved of their anger and fear. May they relax and realize that they are safe. May they heal their pain in a gentle environment where there's nothing to be afraid of.
- May this freezing animal, and all the animals and people in the world who are cold or hungry, be comforted, cared for, warm, and well fed. If there is any opportunity for me to make a difference, let me find it and use it.

Key points of compassionate-insight practice:

- Pause.
- Notice what's happening.

- Feel the tension in your body.
- Feel the sadness in your heart.
- Extend positive wishes to others.
- Switch into a listening space.

ON THE OTHER SIDE OF THE CLOSED DOOR

To transform the roots of aggression—fear and self-doubt—we need to know the difference between the primary, green-light emotion of sadness, and the secondary, red-light emotions created by the racing thoughts and stories of an angry mind. In between, the fear-based vulnerable feelings of the yellow light react to another person's barrier by feeling hurt and misunderstood. To sort through these feelings, we sometimes need to retreat from the situation and create space. The time to do this is right when we realize that a friend now seems like our worst enemy. Being able to hold steady at that point gives us the freedom to try something new.

Lucas's partner, Julie, had a hard time dealing with the pain of being the object of her husband's contempt. All her training in mindful communication was directed toward preventing her own communication light from switching to red. When this happened, she knew that she'd be closed off from her own inner resources, the emotional intelligence of her pain.

Julie heard herself think, *Why is this happening? I didn't do anything wrong.* A neutral observer could have reassured Julie: *Lucas's decision to cut you off has nothing to do with you.* But without that reassurance, Julie's habit, like most of us, will be to take it personally.

When someone else's red-light signal goes on, we face a double challenge. First we need to be careful not to get triggered into our own red-light reactions. Then we need to simply stay present, knowing that communication is closed for now. The key is this reminder not to take it personally, which is hard to remember.

When someone closes the door and puts up a No Trespassing sign, two-way communication has ended. As long as Lucas
is in his red zone, the only reality he is listening to is the story
in his mind. Nothing that is said or done after that point has
anything to do with Julie. The person on the other side of the
door has been turned into an object, scripted into a role in the
red-light story.

Because we human beings are so sensitive to the experience
of being cut off, it isn't easy to accept this. But it is true. Our
friend in the red zone no longer sees or hears us for who we are.
So we have to hold steady with the sadness of disconnection
and keep an eye on the yellow-light fear *What is wrong with me?*
This is when the inner solitude of mindful presence can sustain
us. Using our meditation practice or the support of green-zone
friends, we can stay connected to our sense of basic goodness as
we wait patiently for our friend's communication signal to turn
from red to green again. And this may not happen. Julie's task
was to rearrange the boundaries in her life to adjust to the reality that Lucas was no longer within the intimate circle of her
life. For her, the "For Sale" sign outside their home was symbolic. Without resorting to hatred or aggression, she needed to
envision her former lover moving from her inner space to an
outer, distant circle. This visualization enabled her to grieve the
end of her marriage and to adjust to the new reality that her
lover was now someone who wished her harm.

Julie was mindful that the chain reactions that lead to aggression happen very quickly when communication shuts down.
When someone directs negative projections onto us, it's hard
not to take it personally. When the red light goes on in the
middle of a conversation, we usually either freeze up or see it
like a red cape in front of a bull. For some of us, there is nothing
we want more than to push toward it, trying to break through
the barrier in our relationship. Having an enemy is almost as
passionate an experience as having a lover. We lose sleep thinking
about him or her, our heart pounds at the thought of bumping

into this person in the hall. The momentum is like a powerful undercurrent in a river. We want the last word—and then more.

NO TRESPASSING SIGNS

What happens when someone else's barrier goes up? Being mindfully present at that moment helps us shift into a one-way conversation, with ourselves on the receiving end. Using a journal or in dialogue with a good friend, reflect on the following experiences of being open when someone else is closed:

- Being ignored
- Being falsely blamed or viewed as an enemy
- Being looked down upon, viewed with contempt
- Being devoured by someone who wants to engulf you
- Being set up as a competitor, being undermined for your achievements or qualities or your position of leadership

Feeling the pain of being an object of someone's closed projections, extend empathy to others in the world who are victimized by prejudice, hatred, self-righteousness, and so on. What is the power of staying present without closing down or reacting, and alternatively without bulldozing forward?

SUMMARY

By practicing mindful speech, we break the habit of exaggerating and suppressing and cut the root of the toxic emotions they trigger. It is a method for relating to our red-light episodes with compassion and insight. We deepen our compassion for ourselves and others without sacrificing clarity of mind. Transforming our vision from me-first into we-first is a slow, gradual process of dis-identifying with our masks and becoming more familiar with openness.

It's easier to notice the moments when we feel like defending ourselves than it is to see the ongoing patterns that seem woven into our personality. But we do each other a disservice when we think of these patterns as being who we are. "He inherited his dad's family's temper." "I was born with an addictive personality." It's sometimes hard to separate who we are from the behaviors we learn. An infant may have a genetic predisposition to certain styles of expression, but we don't come into this world with a full set of armor around our heart and a mind full of opinions.

JOURNAL EXERCISE

Comment in your journal or have a dialogue on your thoughts about the key points from this chapter:

1. Look to see what is true. Remember that the red light means trouble. Reactions such as silencing or blaming are really forms of bullying others or ourself. They have no power to protect us.
2. Recognize the various signals in your conversations. In summary these include the following: justifications, refusing feedback, and situations getting worse; the four stages of blaming (complaint, divisiveness, outright blame, retaliation); and silencing or suppressing others and bullying ourselves.
3. Create a time-out or an interruption. Once we see the red light, we act to refrain from causing harm by interrupting the pattern in some way, either by silence, by walking away, or by retreating.
4. Create a "time in-between" for softening by establishing your "green zone." By turning inward we relate directly with compassionate insight to the vulnerable core fears that we've been trying to block.

The practice of mindful speech, which is gentleness, rebalances our patterns of heartlessness and mindlessness. Instead of aggressively trying to push our pain away, gentleness shows us how to live with the tenderness of empathy. Expressing ourselves mindfully exposes our unrealistic expectations. It shows us that we can't possess the people we love, or hold on to moments of joy. As we progress in this training, our emotional reactions become more mature, to the point that we can tolerate the feeling of being misunderstood.

To paraphrase the prayer of Saint Francis of Assisi, when we open from me-first into we-first, our need to be understood dissolves into the need to understand others, our wish to be loved opens into the wish to love others. Becoming selfless isn't like pushing a big rock uphill, trying to become a better person. It's simply opening to the true nature of our heart, to who we really are.

5

The Key to Mindful Relationships
Unconditional Friendliness

Just as a mother would protect with her life her own child, her only child,
So should one cultivate a boundless mind toward all beings and friendliness toward the entire world.
—THE METTA SUTTA,
NALANDA TRANSLATION COMMITTEE

IN THE DUMPSTER behind Olivia Sanford's apartment building is her wedding photo album and a cardboard box full of CDs and letters. "My first choice was to burn them," she said with a smile, "but I was sure they'd catch the whole building on fire. Still, it felt satisfying to heave them into the bin." Olivia's symbolic funeral marked the end of a disastrous relationship with Tom. By tossing her wedding album she was choosing a change of direction, letting go of her habit of "looking for love in all the wrong places." With the support of her mindfulness-awareness meditation practice, Olivia was determined to change her unhealthy relationship patterns and discover the meaning of unconditional friendliness.

When it comes to love and happiness, we human beings want things to stay predictable, to come as close as possible to the romantic ideal of "living happily ever after." We try to possess the people and objects we love, mindlessly ignoring what James Agee describes as "the cruel radiance of what is." Turning this habit around is the focus of our next topic on mindful communication, the key to mindful relationships.

Unconditional friendliness comprises the qualities of openness, trust, and accommodation. When we talk about making friends with ourselves, this is what we mean. This friendship is unconditional because it is more fundamental than the editor in our mind, the impulse to divide things into "I like" and "I don't like." When we activate this friendship, our direct experience of reality—happy or sad, painful or pleasurable—is like a constantly present companion that we can learn to rely on.

Olivia had said good-bye to her unhappy marriage to Tom and was choosing to be alone, to say hello to herself in a new way. She wanted to move past her habit of grasping for security, yet she needed some support. Because she was a photographer, she often expressed her ideas visually. She used a happy childhood memory to envision herself pushing away from a dock and floating down a creek on a rubber raft. We used this image to describe the qualities of unconditional friendliness. What we mean by "unconditional" is open mind, the awareness that recognizes the flowing quality of our everyday experience. And we use the idea of "friendliness" to express tender heart, the ability to feel joy when we're touched by the beauty of what we experience. For we live and love in what Japanese poets call "a floating world."

PRACTICING WITH THE SLOGANS

This visualization of unconditional friendliness was Olivia's version of the reminder to "Go with the green light." She had little flashes of openness when she was meditating, and every now and then they would appear in her ordinary activities. "This morning I discovered that it's possible to wipe the kitchen counter and shine the faucet with the same loving attention that I feel when I brush my dog or stroke a lover's back," she told me one day.

Olivia used the second mindfulness slogan, "When the light turns red, stop," to become more compassionate in understanding her mindless-heart patterns. She didn't want to forget how painful her relationship with Tom had been.

When I first met Olivia, she was staying in a safe house for battered women. Her left eye was swollen and a bruise was forming on her throat. But she insisted that Tom really loved her, in spite of his violence.

"He needs me. We can't live without each other," she said.

I asked her, "Can we set aside the word *love* for a moment and look for another word? For instance, how about the word *respect*? Would you say he respects you?"

She paused and watched the cigarette smoke curl into the space in front of her.

"No, I can't say I feel respected. He never listens to a word I say."

Olivia was used to using mindlessness to adapt to fear-based relationships. Instead of appreciating her own qualities and resources, she had learned to depend on external sources of power. Tom was that source of power for her. Mindless-heart communication patterns were blocking Olivia's discriminating intelligence. Her situation was a dangerous example of how we do this.

In my work with couples, I use the term "relationship cocoon" to describe mindless patterns of relationship. In a relationship cocoon we're seeking a balance of closeness and space while at the same time avoiding what we fear. But when we avoid what we fear, we also avoid allowing ourselves and each other to be who we are. Instead, we turn the other person into an object, a projection, based on our own needs. Relationship cocoons are stuck in a cyclic pattern of heartless-mind and mindless-heart triggered by two opposite anxieties. On one side is separation anxiety, the fear of abandonment that leads to the kind of mindless-heart strategies that Olivia was enacting with Tom. Being dependent, we turn the other person into an object of our craving and give our power away in exchange for security. On the other end of the cycle is the anxiety that may have triggered Tom to shut down his empathy for Olivia. When we feel possessed, or enmeshed, by our partner, we fear the loss of our personal power and freeze that living human being into a threatening object. This is how lovers turn into enemies in conditional friendships.

Although I never met Tom, many of the other men I've worked with experienced the breakdown of healthy boundaries and the feeling of being enmeshed by a woman as a threat to their masculinity. Heartless-mind reactions try to avoid a deep-seated fear of their own gentle, feminine qualities. At the same time, this cycle of mindlessness and heartlessness also manifests in same-sex couples and, as Olivia discovered, it originates from the dualistic barrier that keeps us cut off from our own awake body, tender heart, and open mind. Thus, when conditions change, we might find ourselves on the opposite end of the cycle. This pattern can go on forever as long as we keep moving away from facing our fears and making friends within ourselves.

When we're acting out our fear-based relationship patterns, we lose track of what it means to appreciate beauty and to feel joy. The language we use is deceptive. We confuse the word *love* with emotional hunger and the word *intimacy* with possessiveness. All of this miscommunication begins with a lack of friendliness toward ourselves. We mindlessly grasp onto someone to make ourselves feel better, then we heartlessly push that person away when they're unable to do that for us. When we see this cycle clearly with compassion, we sadly realize how

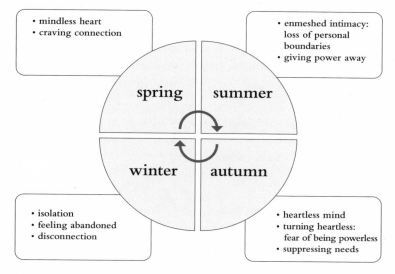

• mindless heart
• craving connection

• enmeshed intimacy:
   loss of personal
   boundaries
• giving power away

spring   summer

winter   autumn

• isolation
• feeling abandoned
• disconnection

• heartless mind
• turning heartless:
   fear of being powerless
• suppressing needs

Fig. 5. "Me-first" relationship cycle.

painful and unnecessary the ups and downs of conditional friendliness can be.

Olivia and Tom's version of this "me-first" cycle was a relationship cocoon called the "pursuer/distancer" game. This strategy tries to balance closeness and space while at the same time avoiding fear. Olivia played the role of pursuer, using mindless-heart scripts, and Tom played the role of distancer with heartless-mind. From a systems point of view, an awkward balance is achieved. Playing these roles keeps the cycle turning, but it also keeps genuine intimacy and personal power out of reach.

As a marital therapist I've seen countless rounds of this cycle of mindlessness and heartlessness. They start with starry-eyed wedding fantasies and often end in grisly divorce-court scenes. As with Olivia, they begin with the mistaken belief that we can find unconditional friendship from our partner rather than from within ourselves. This is a childhood need that doesn't match adult realities. It is an unrealistic expectation that sets us on a collision course in relationships.

Because red-light communication patterns allow us to avoid directly listening to our fears, they keep us stuck. These reactions trigger one another, creating a cycle that blocks the pathway to genuine communication. We see these power struggles not only in couples and families but also in communities and workplaces.

These fear-based relationship patterns depend on speed and mindlessness. When we stop and turn our attention around, making a direct relationship with our own fears and emotional needs, we can discover unconditional friendliness. This is what Olivia wanted to do. Instead of swinging wildly back and forth, she was curious about what it meant to be "alone together"— that is, to be in balance. By learning how to attend to her own needs, she could also turn her attention to the needs of a relationship. Flashes of the green light showed her what happens when we soften and open. She decided to take mental snapshots of this experience when it happened and start a new kind of "photo album" that tells a different story about relationship. Thinking of her wedding album in the Dumpster, she decided to express her recovery by creating a new project, a collage of photos that would tell a different story about relationship, using the vision of we-first.

Seasons of Unconditional Friendliness

Olivia and I worked together to map out the central ideas for her collage project this way: on a white board, we drew a large circle to represent the full cycle of the four seasons of relationship. Then we paused to allow time to reflect and envision what a green-light relationship could look like, with unconditional friendliness as its basis. Olivia decided to create a collage that represented a new kind of photo album that would describe four stages, or seasons of relationship. To gain a deeper understanding and sympathy for her red-light patterns, Olivia needed to compare this new understanding with the painful lessons she'd learned with Tom. So, in the planning stage, she also drew a parallel cycle that corresponded to her cycle of mindless heart–heartless mind. Her intention was to include images in her project that would describe not only the green-light seasons, but also her red-light patterns. At home, Olivia created a series of collages that described her personal journey of waking up from her cocoon relationship pattern into unconditional friendliness.

Olivia used the four seasons as a metaphor to understand the key turning points in healthy relating, as well as the moments that, in the absence of awareness, communication could turn mindless. At each of these stages, there was the potential for a red-light pattern of falling asleep, and there was a green-light antidote she could use to wake up. At first we used these four seasons to broadly map out the direction to a more open and genuine relationship. But later we applied the same key points of mindful communication as guidelines she could follow within her conversations, opening to a "we-first" view.

Here's a summary of what we came up with:

Fig. 6. "We-first" relationship cycle.

Winter: Here, the red-light pattern was to avoid the time and space of being alone. The green-light antidote was to practice meditation and self-reflection. Olivia wanted to look directly at her fear of abandonment and discover unconditional friendliness. By going into her aloneness, Olivia found genuine connection, not only to herself but also to everything around her. In conversations, this is pausing to allow silence.

Spring: The season of Springtime began when something beautiful caught her eye. Her red-light pattern was to grab for it. So, as an antidote, Olivia practiced "window-shopping." We called this a courtship period, a time to gather information without losing track of her intention. In conversations, this is actively listening.

Summer: The season of Summer began when Olivia got what she wanted. This is when the red-light habit of possessiveness surfaced, wanting to hold on at all costs. As an antidote, Olivia shifted her focus to the process of mindful agreements. She wanted to make sure she could follow through with her promises, even small everyday commitments such as showing up on time. She saw this habit as a way of building intimacy and trust. This gave her an alternative to mindlessly trying to control the people she loved. In conversations, this is the practice of expressing ourselves.

Autumn: When the cycle of relationship turns and the good times came to an end, Olivia's red-light pattern was to turn heartless, slipping into anger and blame. Here she needed to let go of her wishful thinking and accept the truth of impermanence, the flowing quality of reality. So her green-light antidote was to let go. In conversations, this is working with disappointment.

Olivia targeted her habit of impulsively leaping into romantic relationships without considering the long-term consequences of her decisions. Mindless-heart patterns place a positive value on Springtime, the time of attachment, and a negative value on the season of letting go. By contrast, unconditional friendliness enables us to find beauty any season of the year. Olivia's new art project consisted of mental snapshots, insights she gained whenever she opened and softened into the present moment, whatever the season. These flashes showed her an alternative to the power struggles she and Tom had been caught up with.

Themes for the four collages that Olivia created for her new photo album, the four seasons of unconditional friendliness:

Winter: aloneness
Spring: new beginnings
Summer: bonding and intimacy
Autumn: letting go

Themes within the four collages that represented Olivia's red-light patterns:

Winter: feeling rejected and abandoned
Spring: grabbing, mindless heart
Summer: making promises I can't keep
Autumn: pushing away, heartless mind

The Winter Stage: Being Alone

Olivia's habit of mindless heart began long before she met Tom. As a child, whenever she felt sad or alone, she turned to romantic fantasy, imagining that her prince would come and give her the unconditional love that she longed for. Her parents were socialites, rarely home at night. Olivia's childish longing for romantic love had been an escape from the loneliness and fear she felt when they were gone. So when Tom said, "I can't live without you," this lonely-child part of her psyche got hooked. This was how she felt too, unable to survive alone.

In her red-light cycle, each time the Winter season appeared and she found herself alone, Olivia slipped into a dark place, torturing herself with the fear that she was unlovable. This happened a few days after I met her, causing her to leave the women's shelter and go back to Tom. "The voices in my head are meaner than he is," she told me later.

Even though her more rational side knew how self-centered he was, Olivia found separation from Tom unbearable. When she tried to break up with him, a predictable pattern began. To overrule her own common sense, she'd drink wine, listen to romantic music, and fantasize about Tom as the love of her life. Then she'd call him and plead with him to take her back. Another round of the cycle would begin again.

In a counseling session Olivia made a drawing of the hungry-child part of herself that was still waiting for her parents to come home. This was her frozen fear of abandonment. She described it like this: "For me, being alone is like feeling abandoned in a cold, frightening, empty cabin somewhere. I feel I could starve to death in a place like that."

Then Olivia realized that she didn't have to stay stuck waiting for her parents to show up. She had within herself the power to warm up that empty cabin and stock it full of groceries. All she needed at first was my encouragement to turn toward her fear of isolation rather than pushing it away. By touching our fears and letting them go, we learn to make ourselves at home in the present moment. This practice of "touch and go" is an important aspect of mindful communication, which we will discuss more thoroughly later in the book. Even people who have suffered traumatic neglect in their early childhood have an intrinsic healthiness that is completely undamaged. Our natural communication system, which connects us to our world, is always connected and ready to kick in.

In the process of creating her photo album collage, Olivia visualized her internal "solitary cabin" as a spiritual retreat. It had a warm fire in the fireplace and plenty of groceries in the kitchen. She reminded herself that aloneness was where she could get to know herself. She realized that such a retreat was essential to her life, and began to look forward to the hour each morning when she practiced mindfulness meditation, had a cup of coffee, and wrote in her journal.

By making room to listen to ourselves, a daily retreat awakens unconditional friendliness to all the parts of ourselves that we normally shun. For Olivia, making room for the pain of her frozen childhood memories allowed her to respond to her suffering with compassionate insight instead of rejection. This was her "aha" moment: "I always used to think it was Tom who was abandoning me. I didn't realize I was doing it to myself." She discovered that the exit point to her red-light cycle was right here, in the discovery that she had the power to become a loving parent to herself.

Sitting meditation practice trains our mind to slow down and interrupt the speed of our thought process. Olivia realized that her fears had no basis in reality. They were like mental movies based on the script "I can't live without you," which triggered a panicky feeling that kept her in crisis mode. But meditation showed her that this movie was just a series of thoughts that became supercharged by her emotional reactions. This insight was an important realization because Olivia's separation anxiety was a key factor that drove her into dead-end relationships.

Olivia's daily retreats also showed her how to expand this unconditional friendliness toward others. She realized that aloneness is necessary in order to breathe fresh air into our relationships. Just as fire needs air, intimacy needs space to rekindle passion and appreciation for each other. Comparing this to her red-light cycle, Olivia noticed that her fights with Tom created this needed space, but in clumsy ways, by cutting each other off for a period of time. Now that she looked forward to aloneness as quality time with herself, she realized that her "winter retreat" was a healthier way of creating space.

You can't see someone clearly if you're up too close or too

far away. So finding the right distance for our relationship boundaries is essential—not too close, but not too far. The amount of space we need varies from person to person. It might have to be wide for one person and narrow for another. But we need to respect the distance between us if we're going to see each other as we are.

In some cases, this distance is created by life situations, forcing couples to adapt to the season of Winter-aloneness. For instance, in Alaska, many of the couples I worked with had one partner who would go out to sea, either to fish or to work on the ferry. The pattern in these relationships allowed for intense time together as well as long months apart. Here's how one of my clients, Carrie, described her experience of forced solitude:

> Whenever Andy goes back to the boat, I begin a process of reabsorbing all the little blames that I normally lay on him. I feel overcome by sadness and regret. At the same time, I become more competent, reclaiming abilities that I'd turned over to Andy while he was here. Earlier in our marriage his being gone so long might have been too intense for me, but at this point it creates just the right amount of space for each of us to taste our individuality again.

It takes courage to investigate our fear of isolation, abandonment, or boredom so that we can touch our loneliness directly. When we go into solitude, even a half hour a day of silent meditation or contemplation, it's possible to look up and see the view outside our window as if for the first time.

Carrie describes this experience:

> Single parenting wasn't easy for my quality time. But when Andy was gone I started getting up really early, at five thirty, to have some quiet time before the kids woke up. I started a journal, but I had no idea what to say. I'd

pick up the pen, but no words came. The first morning as I was sitting there, a little mouse darted by. I jumped and freaked out. But then I laughed at myself. So I started writing about being afraid of a mouse, and the conversation began. I couldn't write fast enough to keep up with my thoughts. After that, I stopped and meditated for a little while. I felt this peace settle within me. The light of the sunrise was filling the room and the little mouse was somewhere behind the wall. I had this feeling of friendliness to everything, that it was all good.

If we practice sitting meditation, eventually the hot, restless boredom and speed of mindlessness begins to relax. We start to appreciate that we can provide contentment and peace for ourselves. Instead of the impulse to grasp something, we develop the discipline to simply let be.

The principles of mindful communication operate at every level of our relationships. We can switch our habits from red to green in our everyday conversations by observing how the "four seasons" turn. For instance, when we pause and deeply listen, this is the Winter stage of aloneness. We allow gaps of silence to naturally occur when our words have reached their limit. Togetherness returns to solitude, we openly listen with nothing to say. Creating this kind of space transforms an ordinary conversation into mindfulness practice.

THE PRACTICE OF CONTEMPLATIVE DSIALOGUE

The winter collage that Olivia created for her we-first photo album project included an image of a compassionate friend. She wanted to remember that she could ask for help in warming up her imaginary retreat cabin. Sometimes we need to borrow the unconditional friendliness from a listener to help us jump-start our own.

I introduced Olivia to the idea of a contemplative dialogue.

This practice is modeled on the way a good friend might try to help us express ourselves and balance our feelings, using inquisitive thinking to cut through the fuzzy habit of mindless heart. Like my friend Ann, a green-zone friend can give us a reality check when we're feeling disappointed or hurt. Normally we feel ashamed when our vulnerable feelings and self-doubts come up. But it's important to ventilate these patterns so that we can see the unrealistic beliefs that hold them in place.

Speaking like this to another person takes courage. It is going public with the very private world of our own inspiration and confusion. So we need to appreciate our willingness to do this. Without the power of mindfulness, our minds are too unstable to understand what we're afraid of. Once we know the difference between the red, green, and yellow lights, we can go toward the original energy instead of turning away from it.

When she was alone, Olivia regarded her journal as her friend, an alternative kind of compassionate listener. Gradually she gained more experience with touch and go, gaining confidence that listening to her fears didn't mean she had to accept them as real. Meditation gently brought her back to reality, allowing her to touch her pain and then let it go into the openness of the present moment.

COMPASSIONATE INSIGHT: SURROUNDING FEAR WITH KINDNESS

Whether we're working with our inner dialogues or external conversations, listening to fear allows a deeper understanding to unfold. This is the practice of the slogan, *when the light is flashing yellow, be careful.* Using her journal, Olivia began to analyze those times when she felt lonely. She used a yellow highlighter to mark the lines that described those feelings. She paid attention to all the ways she tried to cover up her secret fear "I'm unlovable." In the process she became familiar with the self-deceptive beliefs that held that fear in place.

Olivia's five questions to explore her yellow–light patterns:

1. What really happened? Replay the facts.
2. What was the script of my story?
3. What are the messages my body is sending to me?
4. How would a loving friend hear this experience?
5. What is my secret fear? My core self-doubt?

The trigger for Olivia's flashing yellow light was loneliness. Loneliness is a green–light emotion, a very human need for companionship. But when loneliness mixed with her core fear that she was unlovable, it turned toxic. It turned into craving and addiction, driving Olivia to think she couldn't tolerate being alone at home all evening without a reward fantasy, something to look forward to.

To work with her red–light reactions, Olivia needed to catch her story lines at their earliest stage, such as when she's driving home from work and the idea occurs to her that she's going to feel unbearably lonely without a romantic dinner with Tom. Interrupting this fantasy, she sorts out truth from fiction: "It's true that I live alone. It's true that there's no wine there. It's true that I am at risk for loneliness. It's true that it's hard for me to call my friends on short notice." There is a lot to work with, *if* Olivia recognizes her story lines at this stage. A year ago, before she realized that thoughts just meant "thinking," she would be on the couch with a remote control in one hand and a glass of wine in the other before it even occurred to her that she was heading for trouble.

In everyday life, we can meet these core fears during the yellow–light episodes when we feel suddenly stranded. We expect a friendly smile or a word of confirmation from our friend, but instead we're ignored. Our predictable world gets shaky. The anxiety turns into hurt, insult, and worry. We feel exposed and unsafe—or maybe we can't identify what we're feeling. Questions occur. "Did I do something to offend her? Has she grown tired of my friendship?" There is a strong impulse to cover our feelings up. But as long as we feel uncertain, as long as the yellow light is flashing, we haven't yet shut down. We feel ourselves reacting, but we have no idea whether the problem is real or imagined. We are in the *in-between* zone, where friendship could turn cold or open up. If the shock of this groundlessness wakes us from our self-absorption, we might feel compassion for our friend—*I hope she's all right*—rather than insult and paranoia, which is all about *me*.

Mindfulness makes us more resilient when these everyday crises occur. We might remember how unrealistic it is to depend on others' seeing or hearing us accurately. In fact, given how distracted we are most of the time, wouldn't it be better to expect that we'll be misunderstood?

As long as Olivia looked outside herself for solutions, she continued to misunderstand how to relate properly to her root fears. Separation anxiety is one manifestation of the core yellow-light fear *I am unlovable*. We have cut ourselves off from the sources of love within. In the red zone we distract ourselves from this fear by fixating on wishful thinking, which is the opposite of telling ourselves the truth. This is the same instinct as a young child sucking her thumb and dreaming of her mother's breast to soothe her. Our adult version is to focus on romantic rescue or sexual fantasies, or escape into television, food, alcohol, or drugs as a companion.

Our hidden fears give rise to the beliefs and story lines that shape our red-light behaviors. For instance, if our core fear is "I am unforgivable," our script might be "I have to be perfect." Each branch of a root fear has its own story lines. Meditation practice weakens the power of these story lines by interrupting them one thought at a time. We can accomplish the same thing with mindful conversations. To alter a core belief, all you really have to do is see it, be aware of it, and allow your natural curiosity to "reality-test" it. If you truly see a core belief for what it is, even when it tries to run its story, you can't quite buy into it anymore. It's like finding out the owner of your local radio station is a white supremacist. Knowing this will affect your level of trust in that station.

Applying unconditional friendship to our sensitive yellow-light feelings means that we don't get caught in thinking of them as our personal territory. Taking a bigger view, we become curious about the origins of our sense of shame, embarrassment, regret, hurt, insult, irritation—all the rough edges of human relationships. Practicing inquisitive thinking, we turn around and look directly at the chain of misunderstandings that make uncomfortable situations worse. How do these surface reactions suppress the more vulnerable emotional experiences we don't want to feel, such as core fears that we are unlovable, unworthy, or unforgivable?

Olivia realized that letting go of hope for reward, hope for rescue, hope that the love of her life will show up tomorrow didn't mean she would have to sink into despair. "That's about the past, not the future," I reminded her. "Besides, all we have is this present moment." Letting go simply means coming back to things as they are right now. Rather than suppressing her pain or acting it out, she learned how to use compassionate presence to hold her fears with gentle, steady hands.

When we open ourselves to our own distress signals, inquisitive thinking cuts through the confusion of our thoughts like an *aha* moment when we see something we didn't understand before. When we do, the light of unconditional friendliness, which is more fundamental than our hopes or our fears, has a chance to shine through.

Tasks of Winter:

- Work with the flashing yellow light of groundlessness.
- Move toward our fear of isolation, abandonment, and boredom and touch our loneliness directly.

- Practice in solitude, even a half hour a day of silent meditation, to discover the sense of connection to our environment that we've neglected in mindlessness.
- Bring gentle curiosity to our hidden fears.

Spring: Appreciating Sameness and Difference

The second page of Olivia's photo album corresponds with the season of Springtime. This is when we see something beautiful that brings a feeling of joy, like the sight of a yellow crocus after a long winter. When joyful surprises come our way, we want to grab and hold them.

As we've seen, dissolving our dualistic barriers doesn't mean we ignore the natural boundaries of reality. In fact, when we're open, we see them more clearly. This is the lesson of the Springtime season of relationship. My grandmother used to say, "Be friendly to everyone but intimate with only a few." Unconditional friendliness doesn't mean that everyone on the planet belongs in our bedroom. The key to breaking out of mindless heart is to balance unbiased acceptance with inquisitive thinking so that we see who people are and where they fit in our lives.

When Olivia fell in love with Tom, she turned a blind eye to the danger signals. Tom's disrespect for her was obvious to her friends from the beginning of their relationship. "Watch out, he's trouble," her roommate, Ashley, warned. "He says he'll meet you at six and he shows up at eight. When you call him on it, he gets mad and turns the blame on you. Then he shows up with flowers and romances you until you're under his thumb again. I don't trust him." Ashley's advice to Olivia didn't make much difference. Like all red-light patterns, mindless heart is resistant to feedback. We end up walking right past the No Trespassing signs as if they weren't there.

Olivia noticed that when she was in her pattern of mindless heart, the hungry child grabbed anyone who remotely resembled her rescue fantasy. To reconnect with unconditional friendliness in a green-light cycle, she put a photo of a storefront on her Springtime page and called it "window-shopping." She wanted to disconnect the feeling of appreciation from the impulse of wanting to buy.

Spring represents the courtship stage of relationship, associated with falling in love. Passion brings another person intensely into the foreground of our lives and can feel like magic. It brings us out of ourselves, but it's also a powerful intoxicant that few of us know how to really handle. We see someone with beautiful qualities and want to possess him or her. With mindfulness, we can enjoy the powerful energy of love and passion without freezing people into objects of craving.

When the light is red, the courtship stage of relationship can shrink down to nothing. Like a hungry bear, we pounce on the other person as if they were our prey. Conditional love is usually short-lived because we expect the object of our love or affection to meet our needs. This places our friend, child, or lover in an impossible situation. To keep this fantasy in place, we end up giving away more than we can afford.

Olivia and I spent a lot of time talking about how she did this. She mapped out the course of events that followed when she confused the word *love* with *need*. She saw how she handed power over to Tom by slipping into a kind of "toxic niceness" to avoid conflict and criticism at any cost. Suppressing the sharp edges of our experience makes us gullible and easily conned by advertisers, politicians, and pseudolovers of all kinds. When Olivia used niceness, she blindly put her trust in Tom, ignoring the warnings that his red-light signal was flashing.

> When I needed Tom, I filtered out any information that didn't fit with my romantic fantasy of him as being Mr. Right. Then, when I was angry with him, he became Mr. Wrong. He turned all bad, and I couldn't remember anything I liked about him.

In her mindful-communication practice, Olivia decided to exchange her habits of toxic niceness for simple good manners. Another photo on the Springtime page of her green-light album was of a child offering a plate of cookies to guests at a tea party. Underneath this she wrote, "Giving other people the things I want for myself." Olivia used small gestures of politeness toward others like random acts of kindness. The effect was to strengthen her understanding of "we-first" by expressing both self-respect and appreciation.

The decorum of good manners refreshes our relationships even after we have spent many years together. When two partners return home from a day of work, it makes a difference when we create space and time to listen to each other, and to ask, "What were the highs and lows of your day?" Being open to new information gives us a wider lens to see each other in a fresh way. Over time in a long-term relationship, our boundaries start to erode, and we often forget this fresh, "beginner's mind" of courtship. We can restore this by offering an uplifted decorum to each other—as if we're on a first date—and pay attention to little gestures of kindness to remind ourselves not to take each other for granted. In fact, every time we reconnect with each other could be seen as a new beginning, another turning of the seasons.

Being civil and courteous with each other maintains a healthy boundary of aloneness, which is the antidote to mindless heart. At the Springtime stage, we need to keep an even keel of "alone together" so that we don't lose our boundaries, our personal values, and our power. Whether we are two people or two hundred, this balance of "alone" (aware of our individual differences) and "together" (aware of our larger, cooperative vision) is like a flock of geese slowly coming together into a V-formation. The Springtime stage of relationship prepares us for that point when we line up in a single direction. It reminds us that we can both move together even though each one of us has to make the journey alone.

In a workplace or community, the Springtime period is an important time to pay attention to the influences that this new culture will have on our personal values. It begins with our initial application and interview and continues during the training period. Like any courtship, we are usually on our best behavior, nervously trying to figure out how our new coworker or community relationships will unfold over the months and years ahead. The courtship stage is a time to pay attention to small details that may loom large later on. It's important not to rush into a premature agreement without a clear idea of what we want to accomplish together. The same is true of our romantic partners.

The key to the Springtime season is not to compromise our highest values and intentions in exchange for security. Courtship conversations can be blurred by the excitement of connection, like new lovers talking over a glass of wine. So we need to apply inquisitive thinking and explore practicalities. Being clear about our personal intentions and negotiating our bottom lines avoid unnecessary conflict later on.

Another image that Olivia used for the Springtime page of her collage was of a flight attendant. This was a reminder to her to practice mindful speech, clearly articulating her bottom-line values in words, the way a flight attendant makes announcements before takeoff, such as "This plane is going to San Francisco. If this is not your destination, you're on the wrong plane." One of the ongoing struggles between Tom and Olivia had been about her getting pregnant. Olivia was dead set on wanting a child, and Tom was dead set against it. Rather than having power struggles over this topic, Olivia realized in hindsight that her marriage to Tom had been like staying on the wrong plane, knowing it was headed to a destination she didn't want. She couldn't blame Tom for not changing his mind. She had grabbed him without listening, and ended up on the wrong plane.

Olivia wrote in the Springtime section of her journal:

I've tried to capture joy, to possess it like a butterfly in a net.

He who binds to himself a joy
Does the winged life destroy;
But he who kisses the joy as it flies
Lives in Eternity's sunrise.

What does William Blake mean by "eternity's sunrise"? For me, it means touching and letting go of my new friend, this "always present" moment of nowness.

Tasks of Spring:

- Remember the lessons we learned in solitude.
- Bring aloneness into our relationships.
- Touch the joy of Spring and let go into the stage of courtship, feeling the excitement and appreciation for new beginnings.
- Be very clear about what our intentions are.
- Window-shop—that is, look and enjoy, but don't buy what you can't afford.

Summer: Building the Container

The Spring stage only lasts a short while before the Summer thunderstorm season begins. There is a specific moment in time when the season turns. This moment in time is when we make a commitment, officially opening up our boundaries to include someone else. This commitment shifts our focus from "alone" to "together." A commitment is a clear point when we say yes. We decide to accept a job or adopt a pet from the SPCA. We decide to have a baby. We decide to move in with our lover or get married. We decide to visit our Aunt Joan in Missouri, or we decide to meet our friend Polly for lunch at noon.

The key mindfulness practice of the Summertime season is to make this decision clearly and to realize the importance of giving our word. We are making a promise, and our intention is to keep it as best we can. This is how we prove our trustworthiness, allowing the Summer season of intimacy to bloom.

In the red-light cycle, the Summer stage of relationship is enmeshment. When love has no boundaries of aloneness, it turns controlling. We mindlessly control with possessiveness. For example, when my son was a baby, I received this advice from a Zen master:

> Women have a better chance of understanding openness because of their capacity for giving birth. But they lose that advantage when they start treating their child as more special than other children. When that happens, they possess their children as objects, as extensions of themselves.

It didn't take long for me to see for myself what he meant. Not only my child, but everyone I've loved has been caught in my net. Once they are "mine," I want them to conform to my expectations.

Earlier in the book we saw how Paul tried to control his daughter, Mia, confusing possessiveness with love. What Paul learned was that his love for Mia brought up intense fear that he could lose her. The experience of falling in love—with a lover, a child, or a pet—is a joyful surprise that pulls the ground out from under us in a delightful way. We're walking on air, outside of ourselves. The center of our universe shifts and expands to include someone else. But then the fear shows up. We realize that we have no control over the comings and goings in our life. So we create the illusion of control by making our children or our lovers into extensions of our territory. Without realizing it, openness shuts down and fear takes over.

When there's no aloneness in our togetherness, we give away our personal power. For example, Bev and Patrick were married for nine years when their marriage started crumbling. Patrick complained that Bev seemed to be always criticizing him and he could do nothing right. They were spending more and more time apart, and hadn't made love in months.

Bev described the problem this way:

> Patrick doesn't seem to understand how different our values are. For example I'm passionate about recycling. It kills me to use plastic sandwich bags or grocery bags. I'm always turning off the lights. And I don't like eating animals. Patrick is the exact opposite—and he seems to be getting worse, not better. None of these things matter to him. I'm starting to feel like I've lost control over the important things in my life.

Bev's feeling of loss of power was enmeshment. In truth, she'd made choices to give up her values and let Patrick's dominate. During the course of their counseling sessions, Bev and Patrick practiced listening to each other in a deep way. Making room to allow Patrick to express himself, Bev learned to value the differences in their personalities. She commented later, "I realize that I don't have to give my power away but at the same time I can appreciate—not just appreciate, really love—Patrick without expecting him to be just like me." She added with a smile, "What kind of social activist do I think I am when I can't tolerate diversity even in my own home!" It was a powerful turning point for Bev when she turned to Patrick and said, with tears in her eyes, "I'm so sorry for judging you and criticizing you. I see now how toxic an environment I've created for you in this marriage. Please forgive me and let's make a fresh start."

The Summer season is a reminder that genuine intimacy is more about the hard work of surrendering than it is about the pleasure of romantic fantasy. When I perform weddings, I sometimes remind the couple that wedding vows are meaningless when we're in love. They are designed for those future episodes when we can't stand the other person. We need to remember our vow right at the moment when we're about to say

or do something to burn our relationship bridge. One definition of *mindfulness* is "remembering." An inner alarm goes off
right at the moment when we're about to cross a certain line.
We set that alarm when we make our promise, when we gave
our word. But with mindlessness, we ignore the alarm, and the
boundaries get weak.

The wedding vow is a good example of a statement of intention, because for many couples it fades with time. When I meet a
couple for counseling, I sometimes ask them what their wedding
vows were. Many of them don't remember. Olivia said, "It's
strange, I've never thought about it until now. The vows were
beautiful at the time, like my bouquet of flowers. But they were
just part of the ceremony and didn't last much longer." Couples in
strong, resilient relationships regard their promises as living docu-
ments. They've been tested by time, updated as needed, and have
only grown stronger. Instead of a bouquet of dead flowers, their
vows are like a grove of trees that survived many winters.

On her Summertime page, Olivia put a photo of a pressure
cooker, a solid pot with a heavy lid that could handle a lot of
steam. Under the photo she wrote, "Keeping promises creates
a strong container for cooking 'me' into 'we.'"

The vows and promises that mark the beginning of the Summer stage of relationship provide the boundaries for genuine
intimacy to take place. To avoid the trap of toxic niceness, we
need to be able to argue, letting our emotions cook in a strong
container that we can trust. For instance, in our marriage my
husband and I have wrestled through many conflicts, but we've
never had an unfair fight, calling each other names or saying the
one thing that we know will really hurt or frighten the other.
I've also lived in spiritual communities and ethical workplaces
where we strictly follow precepts and communication guidelines. Once we make these agreements with each other, setting
the boundaries, we can build a trusting environment by keeping
our word. Within that container of trust, we can experience our
differences and conflicts without losing a we-first perspective.

The word *commitment* has negative connotations for some people. As the male partner in one of my couple's counseling sessions gruffly said, "I hate the word *commitment*. I always associate it with an insane asylum." The challenge of the Summer season is to be both flexible and reliable. How do we balance the integrity of keeping our promises in an ever-changing climate? Every relationship—even a three-minute love affair with a flower—has a beginning, a middle, and an end.

The commitment stage of a relationship is when family and work obligations heat up the situation and we learn what "selflessness" means. To shift from me-first to we-first, we need to be squeezed a bit. Keeping our word is what gives a parent the ability to care for a sick baby in the middle of the night. It enables a loving elderly husband to patiently feed his disabled wife who no longer is able to recognize who he is.

The health of a family or community depends not only on the trustworthiness of the members but also on having some process of acknowledgment, apology, and forgiveness when trust is broken, as we discussed earlier in the book. It's important to distinguish a green-light approach to keeping our word from the unforgiving red-light approach. As an example, we can look back on the difference between the two styles of leadership that we discussed in chapter 3: the leader who is like the lid of a jar versus the one who is like a gardener.

On her red-light Summertime page, Olivia glued a photo of broken glass. This is what happened in Olivia and Tom's marriage when they replaced promises with controlling rules. Tom's view of failure was brittle: things are broken forever, unfixable. He was preoccupied with control: blaming and retaliating against people who caused him pain, suppressing and silencing Olivia because she described feelings he didn't want to relate to. This is how the Summertime stage turns toxic. In a green-light relationship we keep our agreements out of love and consideration for each other. When there's enough trust in the environment, failures can be seen as learning opportunities.

Another task related to Summer is how to maintain our relationship "container" when we reach our limits. Whenever we make a promise and give our word, we run the risk of breaking it. Olivia contemplated this question for a long time, since her relationship with Tom had consisted of so many broken promises.

For the Summer season collage, Olivia used the image we discussed earlier—of wedding vows or relationship agreements that looked more like a grove of trees than a dead bouquet of flowers. The trees had scars here and there but stayed healthy enough that the roots continued to draw from the soil and the branches reached into the sky. She described this image as, "a balance of being practical but not losing my highest values." Above this snapshot she wrote the word "Forgiveness." We talked about the process of "learning through failure," and compared it to her red-light pattern of either overreacting or underreacting whenever Tom had broken a promise. In her green-light album, she would acknowledge any failure to keep a promise, apologize, and ask her partner for forgiveness. It would have to be an authentic process in order for her new relationship to heal. And she added that forgiveness needed to begin with herself.

Tasks of Summer:

- Letting go of "me" and forming "we" without turning possessive.
- Making a vow, promise, or agreement that offers a reasonable, healthy boundary for intimacy.
- Being flexible and forgiving.

Autumn: Letting Go and Working with Disappointment

In her red-light cycle, Olivia knew that Autumn was the season when she turned heartless. This was when love for Tom disappeared and she hated him, wanting to hurt him. She resisted learning the lessons about letting go. Here's an excerpt from her journal:

Last week my friend Cathy told me that her husband, Ron, had walked out on her. It seems so natural to react by taking sides, making Cathy the good guy and Ron the bad guy. Trying to stay open felt nearly impossible— like watching a football game without choosing a team. I felt like the only option for supporting her was to follow the unspoken rule "your enemy is my enemy." Since then, I noticed that our other friends want to jump on board as well. Everyone has an opinion about who or what is to blame when things go badly.

Olivia had begun to apply inquisitive thinking to her romantic ideas that love should last forever. She saw the belief "Relationships should last forever" as a toxic certainty, blocking the reality that relationships are always impermanent. By diverting their attention onto Ron as a bad guy, Olivia's friends drew their conversation away from the shaky ground of the flashing yellow light, where the sad truth of Autumn reminds us that everything comes to an end.

Olivia contemplated how she had been doing this with Tom, turning this complex, creative, often distressed human being into an object of her passion and her hatred. They both had lost their boundaries in this relationship, seeking intimacy but unable to find it because they confused it with possessiveness. To understand the "harvest" of that relationship, she went back to the seeds she'd planted in the Springtime of their marriage, when she grabbed on to Tom with the childish hope that he would give her the unconditional friendliness she couldn't give herself.

Enmeshment doesn't have enough space for two people to be adults, to stand on their own feet. Instead, Olivia and Tom were trapped in the net of unrealistic expectations. This false intimacy switched to retaliation when Olivia wanted to punish Tom for disappointing her.

Bringing unconditional friendliness to her feeling of disappointment gave Olivia an idea for her Autumn season collage. It was a melting ice-cream cone. In contemplating the image, she envisioned the adult part of herself as her own loving parent, comforting the part that felt like a young child watching the ice-cream cone melt. "I know you want it to last, but ice cream always melts."

To her surprise, she found that she was comforting not only the part of herself that was suffering, but also for the first time she was able to include Tom.

We don't have to take it personally when things come to an end. We may wish we could hold on to things, to possess objects and experiences that we love, but we can't. We wish we could build ground under our feet, pinpoint exactly who we are, but we can't. The choice is ours to see clearly how the real world flows on as it is.

In our conversations, we apply the season of Autumn when we withdraw from "we" by using the "I" pronoun—"I feel threatened when I hear you talk about wanting to move out." We don't need to physically pull away from each other to return to aloneness, but we need to make room for disappointment.

When possessiveness sets in, replacing the touch-and-go quality of genuine intimacy, our friend Disappointment sometime sends us a sharp wake-up call, delivered by the powerful teacher called Death. When my son was fourteen, I had a second child who died during her birth. The experience of being in labor, giving birth, and then witnessing the death of my baby catapulted me out of my normal consciousness. My body, mind, and heart seemed to dissolve into one huge, undivided space that was uncomplicated and awake. My husband and I grappled to adjust to the reality that our daughter's life span had begun and ended within my body. This was her truth, this is who she was. If we loved her, this is what we had to accept. Everything else about her—the nursery we had put together, all the baby clothes and the future fantasies—was a life that existed only in our imaginations. At some point it dawned on me that this experience of love without holding on is the essential teaching the Zen master had told me about years earlier. In the present moment, genuine love completely touches the beauty in someone and yet lets go at the same time.

When we lose someone we love, the cruel radiance of the present moment comes to the forefront. We realize that grief is a natural companion to love. It is a painfully sharp knife that cuts through possessive fantasies and opens our eyes to the truth of impermanence. There is a period in early grief when you see the fragility of life clearly. You wonder why other people are acting so normal. Can't they see that death is right around the corner, ready to snatch the ones we love at any moment, without warning? You glide like a phantom through crowded sidewalks, noticing things that other people don't see. The crumbling edge on the cornerstone of an office building. A tiny flower growing in a crack in the pavement. A flock of geese high above, heading south. You feel like you're in a dream, rather it's more like everyone else is dreaming and you're the only one awake. You feel like shouting, "Death is real, it *really* happens! It will happen! Why do we keep pretending it's not here?"

When we're grieving, we feel naked. It's impossible to hide behind a mask when you can burst into tears anywhere at any time. In the weeks and months after the death of my baby daughter, progress for me meant that I'd find enough time to grip the handle of a shopping cart and focus on asparagus when a new mother would stroll down the supermarket aisle with her baby. On one such occasion, I had this insight:

When you think about how many reasons there are for grieving, how many ways we lose people we love, at this moment, I'll bet at least one in every five people walking through this store is feeling the same sadness right now. And the rest are either healing or about to go through this very soon.

The Zen master would say that this unbiased, compassionate view of our human dilemma was a small glimpse into unconditional friendliness.

Unconditional friendliness comes to us at first in little flashes of insight that interrupt our expectations and show us a bigger picture of the basic goodness and tenderness of our human experience. This is what happened to me when my baby died. But it can happen in less painful ways, such as the mindfulness exercise of looking at a flower for three minutes and noticing how we can shift past the idea of "flower" and instead experience it fully with all our sense perceptions, the way a little child does. These flashes prove that unconditional friendliness is not something we muster up now and then. As a quality of openness, unconditional friendliness is a natural quality of our awareness, like the scent of flowers in the air.

In our relationships, unconditional friendliness is like birth and death happening simultaneously. What dies is the fantasy that other people can be extensions of ourselves, while what is born is the allowing of others to be who they are.

With unconditional friendliness as a ground, we can be realistic about the fact that all relationships appear and disappear in an impermanent world. Even within a single relationship, the cycle turns as we dissolve and re-form again in new ways. The safety net for these transitions comes from knowing how to let go of togetherness and allow aloneness to reemerge. This is the practice of the Autumn stage. It applies to all kinds of endings—leaving a house, a job, a relationship. Like the season itself, it is the time for letting go.

The Zen master's advice pointed to the lessons we learn about love as the seasons turn. As our children become adults, we experience all kinds of births and deaths: the infant disappears into the toddler and the young child into the teenager. When you look at the face of your adult son or daughter, there is hardly any trace of the baby you cradled in your arms so many years before. There was a time when you couldn't bear the thought of being separate from this little person for a whole day, let alone a week or a year. And now it is quite possible that you live in different parts of the country.

Carrie, whom we met earlier in the chapter, described her practice of letting go:

> I remembered the early years of my marriage. When Andy and I had an argument, I used to blame him for wrecking our romance. "Here we were having a beautiful evening and you decided to ruin it by getting angry!" I didn't see at the time that blaming him for his moodiness was no different than blaming the weather for changing. My early ideas about romance were like a childish wish that the days would always be sunny.

Dan and Colleen are a good example of how this season of Autumn happens in small ways within a relationship as we mature from a me-first perspective into we-first:

> I fell totally in love with Dan in the first week that I knew him, and we were living together by the end of that month. Looking back, that first year was tough because he'd have these mood swings that I didn't understand. A few years later the problem became more clear: he'd criticize me for being so messy around the house. I didn't take this well.

As Colleen was reading this aloud, I looked over at Dan, who smiled sheepishly and looked down at the floor. I asked her to go on. "Can you tell me more about what this criticism means to you?"

First of all I don't see myself as a housewife. I'm a creative, artistic person and I admit I use up a lot of space.
What I hear is my mother's voice, scolding me. She was
so obsessively tidy, it drove me insane. She never saw me
for who I really am, for the artist who needs to complete
projects on my own time schedule, not hers. When Dan
walks in, he talks exactly like she did. Reliving her
scolding brings up a lot of pain for me about that.

I noticed how intently Dan was listening, nodding his head
sympathetically. When it was his turn to speak, Colleen was
able to do the same. Their intention to practice mindful communication was evident.

What Colleen doesn't seem to understand is that my
need for the place to be tidy has nothing to do with her
being wrong or bad. It's a deep need that I have for calm-
ness when I come home from a chaotic day at work.

I noticed Colleen shift her posture and lean forward with
interest. Dan went on:

I grew up in a violent, unpredictable environment, and I
know my need for order is irrational. But chaos triggers
anxiety in me at a level I'm unable to relate with at this
point in my life. There's something about an orderly apartment that soothes me. So it's not about her, it's about me.

I saw the expression on Colleen's face soften. She was tran-
sitioning from a defensive child to a loving partner who could
afford to be generous.

Somehow, hearing this makes a huge difference for me.
It feels like the power struggle is over, and instead that
Dan is asking me for a gift. There's nothing I'd love to do

more than to help him deal with his anxiety. I know I can't fix his past, but I'd love to help make his future happier.

When Colleen shifted into a more adult state of mind, Dan was able to do the same:

I know how creative you are and how much space you need. I can live with that, honestly. If we could just agree on some key things, like having the kitchen counters cleared up, I can adapt.

The Autumn stage can even arise within a single conversation. When someone says something that doesn't match our expectations, we touch the sadness of disappointment and then let go, without getting caught in a negative reaction. When we unexpectedly connect with something that someone says, we touch the joyful surprise without trying to hang on. In general, the practice is to let go of our expectations that people be who we want them to be.

Touch-and-go practice reconnects us with the flow of our natural communication system. This flow is the dynamic way that we are both alone and together but never completely isolated nor completely enmeshed. "Touching" is appreciating the beauty of ordinary sensations, such as the smile of a stranger on the bus or the gentle touch of a cool breeze on a hot summer afternoon. "Letting go" means staying awake to the boundaries of reality, the truth that as much as we want to, we can't capture these beautiful moments and freeze them forever. Together, these two instructions provide an antidote to heartless-mind and mindless-heart patterns.

The season of Autumn is an opportunity for harvesting and for generosity. As Dan and Colleen shifted from me-first to we-first, they naturally began offering gifts to each other. The generosity of unconditional friendliness heals our habit of possessiveness by touching lightly and then letting go.

Tasks of Autumn:

- Let go of "we" without resorting to heartlessness.
- Move toward aloneness.
- Work with disappointment and impermanence.
- Create quality time for ourselves.

DECONSTRUCTING DISAPPOINTMENT

Take an example of feeling disappointed and unpack it. Analyze the unrealistic belief that caused it, the emotional expectations. Is there a core fear that "something must be wrong with me?" If so, lean into this fear with curiosity and kindness, like a good friend. Where does it come from? In the light of mindfulness, how real is this fear?

THE FOUR CONFIDENCES OF MINDFUL COMMUNICATION

Olivia's four seasons also apply to four kinds of confidence that we discover by working with fear and disappointment with mindfulness. These are four qualities of a we-first conversation, which is how we express unconditional friendliness in everyday life.

1. *The Confidence of Wintertime:* Mindful presence. Having learned how to care for ourselves properly, we enter a we-first relationship with a healthy sense of ourselves. This kind of confidence is equivalent to having our own autonomy, being able to tolerate differences in points of view without compromising our own values. The features of this stage of conversation include the following:

- Ability to be silent, without interrupting
- Being curious about differences
- Ability to tolerate ambiguity (beyond "right and wrong")

2. *The Confidence of Springtime:* Mindful listening. Because we're at home in our own skin, we're willing to listen for as long as it takes. The confidence of the season of the courtship stage is knowing how to gather information and express appreciation for ourselves and others with an uplifted decorum, as if we were on our first date or a job interview. The features of this stage of conversation include the following:

- Listening to the other with curiosity
- Enjoying beauty with decorum
- Expressing appreciation
- Defining our own intentions
- Finding opportunities for acts of kindness

3. *The Confidence of Summertime:* Mindful speech. The Confidence of Summertime demonstrates our intention to put the welfare of others before our own short-term interests. We prove we are trustworthy every time we follow through with an agreement that we've made. The features of this stage of conversation include the following:

- Negotiating clearly so that the agreements we make are realistic
- Being careful not to give our word recklessly
- Once we say we'll do something, following through
- When we have to break an agreement or a promise, choosing not to just sweep it under the table or justify it, but apologizing and reevaluating what went wrong

Intimacy is the stage when two "I's" become "we," like two lovers making love. But even in the closeness of lovemaking, there is only a fleeting sense of union before the inner solitude of each person emerges again.

4. *The Confidence of Autumn:* Mindful responsiveness. The confidence of responding skillfully is discovered when we let go when change is happening. This is a reemergence of the "I" out of the closeness of "we." The features of this stage of conversation include the following:

- Using the pronoun "I"
- Expressing our differences and negotiating conflicts

The honeymoon ends and genuine selflessness begins when two lovers express their personal preferences and bump into conflict. It could be as simple as one person wanting to go out for pizza while the other wants Japanese food. A we-first perspective is like having a negotiator present to protect the best interests of the relationship when we're working with conflict resolution. Keeping an eye on the bigger picture is an alternative to aggressive impulses of "me-first."

SUMMARY: WORKING WITH DISAPPOINTMENT

In the previous chapter we saw how heartless mind tries to avoid pain by suppressing empathy. Now, in this chapter, we've focused more on mindless heart, which tries to hold on to pleasure by suppressing the clarity of our mind. When tender heart is disconnected from the sharp edges of reality, our boundaries get blurry.

Conditional friendships are unstable because they change like the weather. Intimacy becomes claustrophobic when our boundaries aren't clear. We confuse love with possessiveness. We've discussed how that happened for Olivia. When the light is red, the antidote to mindless heart is inquisitive thinking. Inquisitive thinking is like a good friend who tells us the truth about the big picture. It sharpens our clarity about the details we normally gloss over. It focuses on things as they are, not as we want them to be. It cuts through the notion that the people we love belong to us, that they are extensions of ourselves, and it brings us back to reality.

The time to apply inquisitive thinking is when things don't go as planned. The slogan "When the yellow light is flashing, be careful" reminds us that the in-between feelings of disappointment and hurt contain important information about these mindless-heart strategies, and they give us an opportunity to change them. Disappointment is that flashing yellow light that pops our bubble of wishful thinking and brings us back to earth. It shows up when we have our first fight and our "lucky streak" of being in love comes crashing to an end. New lovers wake up one morning after the intoxication of romance wears off and wonder, "Who is this person in bed with me?" Whenever we feel disappointed, we have an opportunity to let go of our fantasy world and accept people as they are. Including ourselves.

Inquisitiveness isn't criticism. It creates learning opportunities out of our failures and disappointments. It tells us the truth so that we can update our belief system. It rebalances tender heart with open mind so that we can meet our hidden fears with compassionate insight. In particular, it gently unmasks our mindless-heart strategies and exposes the core misunderstanding that there is something wrong or inadequate with who we are, that we're unlovable. By investigating this fear, we discover that it has no basis in reality. We're simply in the habit of ignoring the sources of joy within the present moment, like a hungry child who doesn't know how to feed herself.

In this chapter, we've seen two ways that we block unconditional friendliness with mindless-heart patterns: possessiveness and craving.

When we practice mindful communication, we become acutely aware of the sensitivity of our hearts. Love opens us up, while fear shuts us down. These are the conditions that make friendliness unstable. The communication light switches from green to red before we know it. After a night of lovemaking, your partner wakes up in a bad mood. Or you open the long-awaited letter from the university and read the words "cannot accept you at this time." When life doesn't match our hopes and dreams, the hard work begins.

We connect with unconditional friendliness by relating directly to the fear that shuts communication down. A good place to begin is with disappointment. Mindfulness enables us to use every small disappointment as a training ground for the big ones around the corner.

Disappointment is a toxic-certainty alert. It reminds us that our thinking isn't aligned with reality. Working with disappointment gives us a choice: do we hang on to our opinions and preferences or do we let go? If we choose to let go, hundreds of opportunities to wake up occur every day.

Working with disappointment is the back door to unconditional friendliness. Unlike those warm, sunny days when we're in love, disappointment gives us a chance to relate to the fear or irritation that shuts us down in darker times. We discover that our new lover throws her clothes on the floor or that our teenage daughter is no longer interested in going for nature hikes with us.

We practice unconditional friendliness by gently challenging the misunderstandings that surface when the yellow light flashes. Again, we turn to our friend, inquisitive thinking. We need to reconnect with curiosity and the natural clarity of our mind. With inquisitive thinking, we look closely and analyze what happens when a reaction starts to build; in that way we can recognize our blind spots. For example, you arrive at the bank moments after it closes. That little disappointment called "irritation" can become a fuse that might lead to an explosion with your partner on the way home. Whether or not that happens might depend on many factors—whether or not you had a cup of espresso that afternoon, how easy it was to find a parking place, what the weather conditions in your relationship have been like over the past few days. But regardless of the contributing factors, that moment can either make or break an otherwise peaceful relationship.

Unconditional friendship with our own sensitive yellow-light feelings means that we become curious about the origins of our sense of shame, embarrassment, regret, hurt, insult, irritation—all the rough edges of human relationships. Practicing inquisitive thinking, we turn around and look directly at the chain of misunderstandings that make uncomfortable situations worse. How do these surface reactions suppress the more vulnerable emotional experiences we don't want to feel, such as core fears that we are unlovable, unworthy, or unforgivable?

Feeling cut off from love and joy causes us to reach outside ourselves for these feelings, a choice that always let us down. Sometimes we can notice this playing itself out in the middle of a conversation. This is the microscopic level where the cycle of relationship turns from hope to disappointment in a matter of seconds. When we pause or feel cut off by someone's red-light barrier, we fall from the Summer of feeling connected back into the Winter of aloneness. The shock of suddenly feeling ourselves out in the cold, being on the other side of a closed communication door, contributes to the fear that we're unlovable. It is a flashback to early childhood when being misunderstood by someone we cared about was excruciatingly painful.

Mindfulness brings our relationship issues into the simplicity of the present moment. By opening our mind and softening our heart, we can use disappointment and the other ups and downs of our life as stepping-stones into reality instead of away from it. The key to mindful relationship is realizing that we are always both alone and together. Unconditional friendliness shows us this paradoxical truth. We are born with the ability to appreciate beauty and to love, even though we know we can't hold on to things. Seeing this gives us the courage to genuinely love other people as they are rather than as we wish they could be.

6

The Key to Mindful Responses
Playfulness

In the third stage of selfless help, true compassion, we do not do things because it gives us pleasure but because things need to be done. Our response is selfless, non centralized. It is not for them or for me. It is environmental generosity.

—CHÖGYAM TRUNGPA RINPOCHE

THE INTENTION to communicate mindfully works with all the juicy stuff that comes up between people—love and fear, trust and confusion—and transforms it all into a lifelong path. Along the way, every conversation has something to offer, mirroring back to us what it means to be open, closed, or in-between. We're inspired by a taste of openness, we gain compassion from feeling the pain of shutting down, and we gain confidence by facing the embarrassing, vulnerable "in-between" feelings we normally prefer to hide.

In previous chapters we've discussed how friendliness to ourselves is the basis for communicating more openly with others. We've seen how we dissolve communication barriers by applying the slogans of the green, red, and yellow lights. Now, in this final chapter, we'll turn our attention to the questions that bring us to this work in the first place: How and when do I get the power to genuinely help the people I love? How do I deal skillfully with a person who regards me as his or her enemy? What can I do to make a difference in my family, my workplace, my community?

Having applied these teachings to my life and my work for over thirty-five years, I've learned that the intensity of these questions increases over time along with the dawning realization of how limited we are when we act from a state of mindlessness. We feel like the parent of a sick child, wishing we could help but lacking the skills. At the same time, the more we progress in our mindfulness practice, the more power we gain to genuinely be of help.

By training in mindful communication we gradually make our way through three stages, as indicated by the quotation from my teacher earlier in the book, which we'll look at again here:

> It takes a long time to take our fences down. The first step is to learn to love ourselves, make friends with ourselves, not torture ourselves anymore. And the second step is to communicate to people, to establish a relationship and gradually help them. It takes a long time and a long process of disciplined patience. If we learn to not make a nuisance of ourselves and then to open ourselves to other people, then we are ready for the third stage—selfless help.[1]

We could call the first stage of our path the "red zone." This is when our barrier is up most of the time. We're not yet in a position to help others because we can't hear them beyond the din of our own mind. Although we don't usually realize it, at this stage we ourselves are the sick children, the ones who need help. We're like a patient in the emergency room, in need of loving care. The challenge of this red-light stage of our journey is to stop torturing ourselves and make friends with the parts of ourselves that we've rejected. Some of us spend our entire life in the red zone, a state of mind dominated by paranoia, addiction, or contempt. For others, the red zone is like a case of the flu, debilitating but temporary. The problem is that, like the flu, our red-light reactions are highly contagious. But when we're afflicted by mindlessness or heartlessness, we don't usually realize it. So instead of being cared for in the emergency room, our contempt for others can propel us into positions of influence that spread the toxicity of our personal red zones into our homes, workplaces, and communities.

When we bring our red-light reactions onto the path of mindfulness, we start to notice the contrast between the fever of these intense states of mind and the cool, refreshing breeze of our basic healthiness. Friendship with ourselves begins in that split second during meditation practice when we realize the difference between the dis-ease of our mind, the self-torture of our thoughts, and the simple relief of watching our out-breath dissolve into space.

The second stage of our journey could be described as a "yellow zone." This is the long process of developing disciplined patience by relating mindfully to all the ups and downs of everyday conversations. The goal of this stage is to gain familiarity with the gap—the period in between being open and closed—and break the spell that mindless fantasies and heartless fears have on our mind. We do this by listening to our disappointments with gentle encouragement and gaining insight into the unrealistic expectations we lay on others.

At this stage, we're like the staff of the emergency room, maintaining a basic level of friendliness and helpfulness to ourselves and to each other. For most of us, this level of mindful-communication practice describes the daily practice of observing how we open, how we close, and what happens in between. Like a nurse in the emergency room, we have gained the power to put aside our personal issues and deeply listen to someone who needs our attention. At the same time, we recognize when we've reached our limit, when we're triggered to close down again. We gradually become more patient and less critical with ourselves, and this friendship extends to others.

The final stage of the mindful–communication journey is when we're open most of the time. This is the "green zone," where we're able to selflessly benefit others. We're like the physician in the emergency room, able to diagnose and treat situations that arise. At this stage of our practice we're completely tuned in to the natural synchronization of awake body, tender heart, and open mind, and this gives us the wisdom to respond skillfully to each unique person or situation. Like a physician, years of mindfulness training can result in a single moment when we have the power to save a life. Openly communicating in the present moment enables us to respond spontaneously, like Churchill wagging his tail at the hungry bear.

While few of us may ever achieve this advanced level of being open most of the time, it's helpful to recognize the times when we are. Those are the green–light situations that occur in our lives when we have the power to skillfully respond. Since open communication is we-first, the actions that arise from openness will always be beneficial. To understand this, let's go back to our understanding of the green light and look at three ways that our natural communication system responds to situations, with awake body, tender heart, and open mind.

In a green zone, the awakeness of our body is the energetic relationship that we have with the physical environment around us. It's as though our body is dancing with reality as a partner— the colors, fragrances, sounds, tastes, and physical sensations of our everyday experience. Likewise, our heart is sensitive, able to read the emotional energy of our relationships and to intuitively respond to the needs of others in the same way that we would to ourselves. These responses are synchronized by our curious, open mind, which has a limitless capacity because it is always poised in a state of not-knowing rather than being distracted by preconceived strategies. With these three faculties in play, our natural communication system is in conversation with the energy of the present moment. This is our intrinsic sanity, a self-existing system that is beyond personal territory.

By simply noticing it, mindfulness enables us to cultivate this compassionately intelligent way of responding. Because it has a quality of childlike playfulness, I call this practice "surfing the wave of coincidence."

Surfing the Wave of Coincidence

Ariel is a jazz musician, who describes what it's like to surf the wave:

> At first we are four musicians with different instruments, different sounds. Then we start playing, and something new happens. Riding that energy is like another state of mind that we're part of, but at the same time it's bigger than any one of us. Our separateness dissolves, but we're also hugely awake to one another, to the sound, and were cocreating each moment, not knowing where we're going but always confident at the same time.

Surfing the wave is riding the we-first energy of natural communication. It is cocreated in the present moment. The word *coincidence* originates from the Latin *co* (in, with, together) and *incidere* (to fall on). It is the coming together of two incidents, the activity of the present moment that arises from multiple encoders. It is during those brief intervals when we mindfully open to the present moment, undistracted by thoughts about the past or the future, that we cocreate a response to situations. When an enemy approaches, we might cheerfully wag our tail because we're naturally unbiased, without personal territory. The automatic impulse to shut down is gone. Instead of following a personal script, we stay tuned to the coincidences of nowness, which give us information about what to do next. My teacher describes this as being able to recognize the choice that is already present in a situation: "If a person realizes that a whole chain reaction of incidents brought him into the present situation, that solves a lot of problems. It means that you've already made a commitment to whatever you are doing and the only way to behave is to go ahead, rather than hesitating constantly in order to make further choices."[2] For Ariel and her friends, that choice is the next note they will play, codiscovered by their mutual energy rather than by any one of them alone.

We can trust this wave of coincidence when we're communicating openly in the present moment. When our sense perceptions, empathy, and natural clarity of mind are available, we're poised to be of help to others. In contrast, mindless attempts to be helpful often miss the point. This is a tricky subject. A general guideline that we can follow is laid out in the well-known Serenity Prayer. It reminds us that compassionate action needs to be guided by wisdom.

> *Grant me the serenity to accept the things I cannot change,*
> *The courage to change the things I can,*
> *And the wisdom to know the difference.*

"The serenity to accept the things I cannot change" comes from mindfully allowing people and situations to be what they are. We gain this power by applying the slogan "When the light turns red, stop," curbing our impulse to react when we feel uncomfortable.

"The courage to change the things I can" comes from working with the groundlessness of the flashing yellow light, moving toward our fear instead of away from it. As we've seen, the power to transform our very sense of who we are lies within these gaps of uncertainty.

The third point is key to our present topic. We develop "the wisdom to know the difference" by mindfully observing how we open and close and thereby becoming more familiar with the selfless qualities of the green light. In the emergency-room analogy, we've gained an understanding of the difference between health and disease, and we're now able to apply the proper antidotes.

The roots of this wisdom have been with us from the beginning. Newly born infants have the intelligence to spit out poison and take in food. This is the wisdom of awake body. Likewise, our open mind has a truth detector that intuitively knows the difference between fact and fiction. Our tender heart has a lover's instinct for genuineness, to communicate with soft, naked skin, not with a suit of armor.

Although we are born with this green-light way of knowing, we lose this natural synchronization when we're controlled by unconscious fears. Me-first reactions focus mainly on our own emotional hunger and defenses, without much concern about the impact our needs have on the social environment. In this sense, mindful communication brings our attention back to the social ecosystem that we are part of. When we're tuned in to this bigger sense of body, heart, and mind, our natural wisdom is activated.

Mindfulness training teaches us the wisdom to ride the energy of our lives properly by keeping the balance of awake body, tender heart, and open mind. The key is playfulness, a flexible creativity that isn't trapped by conventional thinking or preconceived ideas.

The Power of Awake Body

The first and easiest waves to catch are the coincidences that come from the physical environment, the naked perceptions we observe without interpretation. Awake body tunes us in to the coincidences in the physical environment, the play of the elements, and the forms and gestures that speak to us. British artist Andy Goldsworthy is an example of this. He creates dynamic works of art in partnership with nature. Andy carefully shapes forms out of ice and delicate nets of grass. When the ice melts or the grass blows away, nature has added her contribution. His artful conversation with nature goes both ways.

Transformative conversations are like this. They lift us up and carry us into the unknown. Unlike red-light communications, which are blocked by preconceived expectations and agendas, the space of not knowing what to do or say can lead to a very specific action or expression.

Like my friend Martina, skillful responses can uplift others without words. To understand how to surf the wave of coincidence is to explore how we communicate by playing with the elements of the environment. These silent conversations can be simple statements; for example, my husband creates a clean and inviting empty space in the dining room, and I respond by putting a branch of autumn leaves in a vase on the uncluttered table.

An example of the power of awake body is a scene from an old Japanese film, *The Seven Samurai*. As the story unfolds, we see a stranger traveling alone through a lawless village. But this stranger is not an ordinary man, he's a wandering samurai. We see him calmly eating a bowl of rice with his chopsticks, apparently oblivious to the danger outside the back door, where a gang of thugs is gathering like wolves surrounding an isolated sheep. The attackers are moving stealthily to the open door and are about to launch their ambush. The afternoon air is still, except for the drone of flies in the kitchen. Without moving his eyes the samurai's attention scans the room like a beacon. Then, in an instant, with uncanny smoothness, he casually plucks a fly from the air with his chopsticks. He holds it gently, as if studying it, then lets it buzz away unharmed. The gangsters at the door gasp, then run away in terror. The samurai's eyes meet those of the innkeeper, and the two of them break into laughter.

This simple gesture reminded me of a time when my teacher handed me a pen. His hand made an arc with such gracefulness that it stopped my mind. When I started to pay closer attention, I realized that every movement he makes has a similar artfulness.

Co-creativity: The Elements at Play

To learn more about the waves of coincidence in our physical environment, it helps to spend time alone in a natural setting. In silence it's possible to open up all our senses and really listen to the world of nature. We feel an inexpressible joy in response to the play of the elements: water tinkling over rocks, sunlight dancing on the waves, the high-sailing clouds turning pink in the sunrise. The wisdom of our own spontaneity is similar to this play of the elements in the natural world. Like air, water, sunlight, and earth, we realize that our relationships with other people are not solid, predictable things. They are fluid experiences that are always interacting and emerging in the present moment. When we're communicating openly, the elements of our individual personalities blend with the other person's and create a unique new molecule, like oxygen joining with hydrogen to make water.

Mindful responsiveness plays in the open space of not-knowing like a rainbow appearing in the sky. We learn to play with coincidence.

The Power of Tender Heart

The second way of surfing the wave of coincidence is by trusting and acting upon tender heart. As we discussed earlier, green-light emotions are awake and intelligent, whereas the opposite is true of red-light emotions. By listening to the emotional themes within a conversation, we can learn how to distinguish between open and closed, and tune in to the unspoken fears that often lie in between. The emotional content tells us what we need to do to meet our own needs as well as the needs of others. If the person we are listening to is in a red zone, we can bring to mind the analogy of the emergency-room patient, knowing that our own needs can't be heard. If we are able to listen openly, the felt experience of directly touching our own hopes and fears will translate into knowing the hopes and fears of others. This empathic way of knowing arises as compassion, joy, love, and sadness—even anger, under some circumstances. Because they aren't centralized or generated by our own internal stories, they have nothing to do with personal territory. Instead they are we-first responses to the needs of relationship or events in the external environment. So the actions that follow from them are appropriate. Here are some examples:

RESPONDING TO FEAR BY OFFERING PROTECTION

In April 2011 a British tourist named Helen Beard who was visiting Florida received the local sheriff's office's medal of merit for heroism. She was being rewarded for running from the side of the pool when she spotted a one-year-old girl dangling from a fourth-story balcony. She positioned herself below so that she was able to catch the child when she fell. When she received her award, she said, "It feels a bit daunting to be here for something that was instinctive. It felt like it was something anyone would have done." She added with a smile that she was simply glad she'd been wearing her flat shoes that morning.[3]

When we're open, the intuitive response to someone else's fear is to feel the fear ourselves and use that adrenaline to offer protection. Countless examples of this kind of heroism, where strangers risk their lives for others, demonstrate that our human nature is fundamentally we-first.

RESPONDING TO PAIN WITH COMPASSION

My friend Sean offered this example from his own life:

> I was driving my Cadillac down the street one snowy day when I noticed an elderly couple ahead of me, walking along the sidewalk. Right at that moment, the woman slipped and fell to the ground. Her partner looked pretty unstable himself. I pulled over to see if I could help. I watched the old man trying to pick his wife up, but it was clear he couldn't do this. I felt overwhelmed with sadness to think of how powerless he must have felt. So I got out of my car and went over to him. I stood behind him and supported him so that together we were able to get his wife up to her feet.

Sean's compassion shared not only the pain of the elderly couple but also intuitively responded with a skillful solution that would empower the elderly gentleman rather than push him aside.

Because green-light emotional messages are we-first, they give us not only information about a problem but also clues about the solution.

RESPONDING TO LONELINESS BY CONNECTING

Michelle, who volunteers at a hospice, tells this story of surfing the wave of coincidence:

> I was visiting Makiko, who was a widow with no family in Canada. She had left her native Japan decades ago and was living alone before she came to the hospice. She was still able to walk, but feeling depressed. Down the hall, by coincidence, we had another patient, named Dori, who was also from Japan, and her room was always full

of family members, who brought her boxes of Asian food every day.

Feeling the sadness of Makiko's loneliness, it was obvious to me that these two residents needed to be introduced to each other, though normally this isn't something I would want to do. So I persuaded Makiko to go with me for a walk down the hall and by chance we met Dori's sister. It didn't take long for Makiko to be adopted into their family and offered food and conversation in her native Japanese.

As my teacher said, the right choice is in front of us, and sometimes, as in Michelle's case, it is easy to see. But without tuning in to Makiko's unspoken loneliness, Michelle wouldn't have taken the risk to do something about it.

RESPONDING TO GRIEF WITH COMFORT

Earlier in the book I described the story of listening to Betsy's depression and feeling the sadness of grief. In her case, she was suffering from depression, and I recognized this because of my personal experience. But as a psychotherapist it has happened many times that a client who comes to me describing depression is in fact suffering from bereavement. One example was Maya, who felt hopeless, had no appetite, wanted to sleep all the time, and was tearful for no good reason. When I asked, "Have you had any significant losses in the past few years?" she at first said, "No, everything's been fine." But then she paused. "In the past few years? Well, my dad died five years ago. I know I should be over it by now, but I'm ashamed to say I'm not."

Depression is a secondary reaction that is characterized by toxic thinking, self-hatred, and despair. Bereavement is not an illness, but because many people don't receive support and education about the process of grief, people like Maya end up not knowing how to ask for the comfort and support everyone needs after we've lost someone we love.

RESPONDING TO HAPPINESS WITH CELEBRATION

I was walking through a large shopping mall one day when I heard a cheer. I looked over to see a small circle of people gathering. Curious, I made my way to see what was going on. In the center of the circle was a young couple and an empty stroller. In the space between mom and dad a tiny child in a bright green playsuit was taking her first steps. Everyone clapped their hands. Sharing the joy of others, we smile. It's natural to respond to happy feelings with celebration.

RESPONDING TO ANXIETY WITH ACTION

Here's another story that Michelle shared from the hospice:

> Rita was depressed about a long-standing problem with her brother. She hadn't talked to him in thirty years. During our conversation the idea arose that she could write him a letter, with my help. She wrote the letter and felt great relief. She died the next day.

Michelle was trained to simply listen to the patients, without adding her personal agendas. But in the course of openly listening, the distress signal of Rita's anxiety sent an emotional message that Michelle received and acted upon. Like depression, sometimes what appears to be anxiety is a signal that there is a problem that can be solved by immediate action if we know how to listen.

The Power of Open Mind

The third function of our natural communication system is open mind. The key word for open mind is *curiosity*. To paraphrase a famous teaching from one of the Zen patriarchs, "The way is easy for those who cease to cherish opinions." A green-light conversation is a journey of discovery in which one story un-folds into another. One of my teachers says that he practices this on airplanes. "If I have a chance to talk with the person sitting next to me, I'm curious about where that person's pas-sion in life is. So I keep asking until I find it." A few weeks after he told me this, I tried it for the first time. The woman sitting next to me was heading for a human-resource manage-ment conference in Las Vegas. We chatted a bit about this, but my curiosity wanted to probe further. What were the things she really loved to do? It didn't take long to discover her pas-sion for dancing. When she spoke about her lifelong love of dancing, everything about her way of communicating changed. Her gestures became more fluid, dancing in the air. Her face became more animated and colorful. By the end of the short flight, both of us felt invigorated.

Surfing the wave of coincidence with open mind adds fur-ther dimensions to our conversations as we explore the layers of story that each human being brings to a single moment of ex-perience. When we hear each other's stories, we often find our way out of dead-end conflicts. So much conflict and miscom-munication is traceable to simply not making the time to learn more about each other. As one of my teachers said, "We're all living in our own world, as if we're tuned in to different radio frequencies. It's a miracle that we can communicate at all." Open mind doesn't assume that we know what the other per-son is saying. It is a humble process of wanting to know more.

One thing I've learned over the years is that we need to put in some effort to create opportunities for these kinds of conver-sations. We need social green zones where we can have the time and space to deeply listen with open mind, tender heart, and awake body. When we engage with one another this way, we experience what physicist David Bohm calls "transforma-tional dialogue." Transformational dialogue is different from an ordinary approach to problem solving. Normally we start off not-knowing and then gain information so that we feel certain. This kind of learning is practical and very helpful in our lives. But transformational dialogue is the opposite process: we begin with some ground under our feet, but then we leap and enter the open space of not-knowing. It is here in this not-knowing-space that the magic of spontaneous wisdom occurs.

RESPONDING TO AGGRESSION WITH COMPASSION

People often ask if mindful communication has its limits. Even if our view of human nature is that we are basically good, this doesn't mean that dangerous people won't come into our lives. It may happen that when we look with open mind, what we see is someone who regards us as an enemy. Not all hungry bears will respond playfully to our green-light signals. In difficult relationships, how do we walk the fine line between accepting what we cannot change and changing what we can?

A situation like this happened to Zachary. One of his co-workers, Lisa, was the sister of Zach's college girlfriend, Tamara. When Zach broke up with Tamara, she went on a rampage, throwing his stuff out the window and raging about him to her friends. Lisa had vowed revenge to her sister, and now, years later, she found her opportunity when she discovered that Zach had recently been hired in the same division where she worked.

Zach's first clue that he had a problem occurred when someone he just met said to him, "Yes, I've heard about you." Over the next few weeks, he felt an unnerving disconnection between the things he said and the way that certain people in the office reacted to him. Finally, the situation came to a head when he ran into Lisa, who glared at him. "I'll make you pay for what you did to Tamara. I plan to make your life as miserable as you made hers."

Zach felt powerless in the face of Lisa's contempt for him. He wanted to deal with the situation as mindfully as possible.

So the first step was managing his own red-light reactions. In chapter 4 we focused on preventing our aggression from flaring up in situations like this. Refraining from acting out is an essential first step before we can be skillful in dealing with someone else's aggression. So first, we use mindfulness to interrupt the tendency to react heartlessly with complaint, divisiveness, blame, or retaliation.

To remain we-first, Zach was determined not to speak negatively about Lisa. He made the intention not to defend himself by harming Lisa's reputation, building a case against her, or by freezing her into a role in his own story line. By stopping these red-light behaviors, Zach prevented his own reactions from turning heartless.

Zach's second step was to make sure he didn't turn aggression against himself, suppressing the intelligence of his green-light emotion by silencing his truth. He had a tendency to go in the direction of mindless heart, pretending that everything was fine when it was not. So he stayed in touch with the emotional energy in his body and acknowledged the painful effects he was feeling from Lisa's hatred of him. "It's hard to wake up in the morning and feel dread about going to work. I'm aware of feeling hurt, sad, fearful, powerless, and angry that Lisa hates me so much."

Mindfulness meditation gave Zach the serenity to accept the truth that he had an enemy in the workplace. By holding a we-first intention to communicate openly, he aroused the courage to change whatever he could. Bringing awake body, tender heart, and open mind into his communication with Lisa enabled him to discover the wisdom that knows when to act and when not to act.

In the tradition of mindfulness, there are four progressive stages of compassionate activity that occur when we stay open. These stages parallel the four confidences of mindful communication and can be applied to problem solving or conflict resolution.

1. *The compassionate activity of pacifying:* The first step in dealing with someone else's aggression is to hold steady with our own serenity, like a peaceful lake that can reflect back the sky and trees around it. We express this mirrorlike clarity by describing the problem or situation accurately to ourselves, without exaggerating or speaking in generalizations.

2. *The compassionate activity of enriching:* The second step is seeing the gold, or goodness, in the situation and making an offering of generosity to our opponent. We recognize that all aggressive action is based on inner feelings of inadequacy. In a conflict, when our opponent is engaged in the seesaw pattern of divisiveness, enriching actions can sometimes level the playing field and invite our opponent into a cooperative stance. Zach's "offering" to Lisa was to remain curious about who she was, to listen for alternative stories, noticing and appreciating any positive quality he found in her within the present moment. To enrich a challenging situation, we often need to absorb insults and emotional injuries while waiting for a flash of openness to occur in the other person.

3. *The compassionate activity of magnetizing:* If the opponent doesn't respond to the second stage of enriching, we need to draw in even more power and resources. When there is a warm, bright fire in the fireplace, people are attracted to move toward it. Unconditional friendliness gives us this kind of power. In Zach's workplace, even though he was new, he trusted the basic sanity of his fellow employees to recognize that he was not the person Lisa was making him out to be. By not responding to her aggressively, Zach radiated gentleness. This attracted his coworkers, and finally their supervisor, to pay closer attention to the problem that was beginning to affect the whole environment.

4. *The compassionate activity of cutting through:* The final stage of a compassionate response, when the previous three stages have had no effect, is to abruptly remove the obstacle. To respond like this without aggression takes the skill of a surgeon who can use a scalpel to delicately remove a brain tumor or the

skill of a samurai who defeats his enemies by gently plucking a fly from the air with his chopsticks. Cutting through is an unpremeditated, completely awake action, like an Aikido master who can step aside at exactly the right moment and let the weight of aggression fall on itself. Often the wave of coincidence takes on a life of its own at this point, and by simply holding steady, other forces come into play to resolve the situation. This is what happened with Lisa's bullying behavior. When Zach held his own composure and maintained a we-first perspective, the nature of the communication breakdown became more apparent. Lisa blundered when she tried to sabotage a major project Zach was working on. The end result of her own actions was that she was given a reprimand and put on probation.

These four stages are four ways that we respond to situations without reducing them to the personal territory of me-first. Like the four seasons of relationship, they follow a natural evolution. Many communication problems are clarified at stage one. Coming back to the openness of the present moment and applying mirrorlike listening, we gather a fresh understanding of the situation. The sources of information are awake body, tender heart, and open mind.

SUMMARY

Awake body: Open up, come back to the energy in your physical body, and listen. Expand your attention to the physical environment, notice the colors, shapes, sounds, smells, and textures in the room. Allow your senses to take in the nonverbal messages from the other people in the room, their expressions, posture, gestures.

Tender heart: Open up, let go of words, stay present in your body, and feel the energy in your heart as it sensitively detects the emotional weather patterns of the room. When your mind gets hooked by an interpretation ("I can see that Joe's feeling a bit nervous about this meeting"), touch that lightly and let it go. Stay tuned to your own emotional reactions without losing the connection to the atmosphere in the space. For example, you might mentally note, "Fear . . . sadness . . . anxiety . . . warmth . . . humor."

Open mind: With curiosity, we touch and let go of the insights and understandings that arise in our mind. Bringing words to the mirrorlike reflections of our awareness, we describe the situation with as much accuracy as possible.

By mirroring the details of the situation, both inner and outer, we become aware of the subtle ways we can distort information simply by our choice of words. For instance, Lisa told her supervisor that the problem was a conflict between Zach and herself. But by mindfully paying attention to the details, her supervisor realized that the situation didn't correspond with the word she'd used, *conflict,* which implied that both parties were involved. Later it was agreed among the team that the true problem was harassment, a one-way situation, with Lisa bullying Zach.

The world can never be perfectly managed, but we can make peace with our lack of peace, learn to live with it, feel it, swim in it. If we're searching for a perfect world other than the one in front of us, we're lost in daydreams. Instead, when the flow of experience brings something we don't like, we don't have to slam the door shut. By training ourselves to hold steady with mindfulness, we can learn to genuinely accept ourselves and others as we are and, at the same time, respond skillfully to the challenges that block communication.

Humor and playfulness: The main quality of skillful action is that it has an element of humor and playfulness even though it can be emotionally painful. Playfulness comes from regarding the present moment as our dancing partner, our lover, our constant companion. This present moment is, in some inexplicable way, in a different dimension from the past or the future. Conversations that arise from nowness are alive and open.

You can feel this openness diminish when we drift into past or future stories. Like Lisa, when we're gripped by resentment from the past, our communication lines to the present moment are down. I noticed this in particular at the end of a long silent group retreat. Three of the other women and I were in the kitchen quietly chopping vegetables on the day the retreat ended. We'd become so accustomed to silence that it didn't occur to us to speak. Then Jane said, "Hey, retreat is over. We can talk." We laughed a bit nervously, and gradually words came. Our first conversations focused on our immediate experience. "Look, out the window, can you see that heron flying off in the distance?" Later, one of the women, Kathleen, drifted into stories of the past. "I remember years ago when I lived in California . . . do you remember those days when our kids were young?" The mood shifted. It was neither good nor bad, but you could feel the energy of the present moment shut down as we reconstructed the familiar stories and reference points that shaped our identities. Thinking of the past, I felt a welling up of sadness. Then our conversation moved into the future, about our plans after the retreat. Again there was a shift, this time accompanied by a tightening feeling of excitement mixed with anxiety.

This phenomenon is pointed to in the teachings from the mindfulness traditions: when we talk about the past or the future, it's easy to generate emotions of nostalgia and anticipation that aren't grounded in reality. When these thoughts become fixated, sadness freezes into depression, and future fears trap us with anxiety. Like daydreams, our memories and fantasies are no different from the thoughts that arise in meditation, drawing our attention away from the present moment. To practice responding mindfully, we need to gently pop those bubbles of past and future, tune in to the awakeness of the present moment, and listen for clues about what needs to be done next.

In Closing

The principles of mindful communication that are being presented here are shaped by contemplative psychology, the study of the mind through meditation. In the early 1980s, when I was studying Buddhist and Western psychology in graduate school, I wondered why we weren't being given more specific tools and techniques to use in our work. My professor, Dr. Ed Podvoll, replied that psychotherapeutic tools and communication formulas are readily available and easy to learn, but that the perspective offered here was harder to find. These principles that describe open communication, gained from the direct experience of meditators over thousands of years, are rare and priceless. For this reason, in this book I've chosen not to emphasize communication skill-building techniques such as assertiveness, nonviolent communication, or conflict resolution training, which are available in many books and programs on the market today.

In my professional work as a psychotherapist, administrator, and as the leader of Gampo Abbey's three-year retreat center, I've applied these principles to the dynamics of relationships with couples, families, workplaces, and spiritual communities. In this book I've chosen to focus on the subject of communication because our conversations reveal patterns of kindness and fear both in our relationships and in our society. Meditation adds another perspective that shows us how the inner conversations we have with ourselves determine how much friendliness we bring to others.

I'm convinced that these keys to mindful communication have the power to restore peace and harmony in our society. I use the word *restore* because at some fundamental level this harmony is our starting point. If human beings were not basically we-first by nature, conflict would not feel painful. When a healthy body feels pain, a message is being sent to pay attention. We can regard the pain of the red light in the same way. The crises of the twenty-first century are based on patterns of greed, aggression, and mindless exploitation of our own resources. The suffering of these dead-end patterns urges us to shed the false idea of me-first at every level of our experience and to deepen our sense of interdependence.

Another reason for writing this book is that I've personally seen that even in the most ideal of circumstances—such as a group retreat dedicated to compassion and selflessness—it is difficult for these instructions to take root in our conversations. These teachings remain empty ideas when you divorce them from the nitty-gritty stuff of our own human journey. In our work together, Olivia and I came to agree that the rugged ups and downs of people's life stories don't fit into tidy photo albums. Our lives are a tapestry of love and loss, doubt and clarity. The privilege of being able to work intimately with so many other people has taught me that every human life is a work of art that deserves recognition.

In closing, here's an overview of the five practices of mindful communication we've described:

1. *The keys to mindful presence* are awake body, tender heart, open mind, which are the three components of our natural communication system. The practice that trains us to reconnect with these qualities is mindfulness meditation, which enables us to positively interrupt all the ways we distract ourselves with expectations, story lines, and emotional reactions. These distractions create the illusion of me-first, the need to promote or defend ourselves, which is the obstacle to being mindfully present here and now. Like Olivia's season of winter, meditation practice is how we make friends with ourselves by creating the space to simply be who we are. Within this undistracted inner spaciousness, thoughts are free to come and go, emotional reactions naturally resolve into tenderheartedness and our sense perceptions awaken a sense of connection to the environment around us. This is how the barrier of mindlessness

dissolves and we learn to rest in the present moment, symbolized as the green light.

2. *The key to mindful listening* is encouragement, the ability to see through masks and spot the golden qualities in a person. Like Jack Norton, a benevolent mentor, therapist, leader, or parent is like a gardener, bringing these golden qualities forward and cultivating them. The practice is to deeply listen to others with the view of unconditional positive regard, taking delight in the gifts they bring to the world. The obstacle to encouragement is toxic certainty, the false confidence of self-righteousness, which propagates discouragement and inferiority in others. We overcome this obstacle by shining the light of encouragement inward and dispelling our own inner sense of unworthiness. Then we can positively influence others by leveling the playing field and seeing ourselves in others.

3. *The key to gentle speech* is gained by learning to speak in a way that allows us to be heard. The practice is refraining from causing harm with our words by learning to stop when the light is red. To do this, we need to make a relationship with the obstacles, all our red-light signals, such as the four stages of heartlessness. Instead of focusing on external enemies, we look inward at the self-deception and justifications that cause aggression. Working with the slogan, "be careful when the light is yellow," we distinguish between aggression and the original pain—the underlying fear and self-doubt that call for kindness and insight, not rejection. Understanding the roots of aggression gives us the power to interrupt the momentum of negativity in our conversations by gently refraining from exaggerating or minimizing and keeping the listener in mind.

4. *The key to mindful relationships*, unconditional friendliness, is a path of intimacy that unfolds as life's seasons turn from aloneness into togetherness and back into aloneness again. The mindfulness practice is called touch and go, making room for both joy and sadness to be present in the flow of our moment to moment experience. Genuinely appreciating the beauty of

other people without attaching them to "me" is how we exit from the cycle of heartless-mind and mindless-heart, the relationship cocoon that is the obstacle to mindful relationships. In a mindless cocoon we try to insulate ourselves from loss by clinging to relationships as permanent things. This mistaken view leads to conditional friendships that swing from too close, triggering heartless-mind reactions, to too far away, triggering mindless-heart patterns. Restoring the balance of open mind and tender heart gives us a basis of unconditional friendliness that brings all of our conversations, even antagonistic ones, onto the path of mindful communication.

5. *The key to mindful responsiveness* is the playfulness that arises when we're open, unburdened by preconceived ideas and strategies. This is the path of the artist whose intention is to express the beauty of human experience, a heroic beauty that can be found even in the midst of tragic circumstances. The mindfulness practice to develop the power of playfulness is called surfing the wave of coincidence, a practice of entering situations with no agenda other than to be of help and listening for clues as to what to do or not do. The obstacle to responding mindfully in the present moment is to be distracted by strategies based on preconceived ideas from the past or ambitions about outcomes in the future. All kinds of controlling behaviors block access to the playfulness of the present moment. Letting go of these controls and opening to the messages from awake body, tender heart, and open mind, we enter a conversation with all the elements in our environment and learn to dance with the energy of the present moment.

These five keys can be found in our own experience along the path of mindful communication. I hope that the contemplations and journal dialogue exercises have made it more possible for you to explore your own version of this path. By focusing primarily on communication—the process of relationship—we can go to the heart of human joy and sorrow, the source of emotional wounding as well as of emotional healing.

The view offered in this approach to relationship is optimistic. The power to communicate openly may seem like the final destination of a long journey, but at the same time, this destination is also our home ground, the place from which we start. What we call the green light, or openness, is a quality of our true nature that we discover by simply relaxing and making a relationship with the ordinary experiences of everyday life. The length of the journey depends on how long it takes to become confident enough to let go of our pretenses, especially when we're challenged by difficult relationships. The five powers are gained by working with these challenges. In mindfulness practice we're always moving forward, because we learn just as much from failure as we do from success.

As human beings, we depend on language. And this is why we need to develop new ways of talking about the changes in perspective gained when we mature from relationships based on wanting our own needs to be met to relationships that have the intention to meet the needs of others. Helping you to set out on this journey from me-first to we-first is one purpose of this book. The broad principles and system of ideas offered here are intended to point to and clarify the subtle shifts in our psyche that make the difference between joy and suffering in relating with others. Being present for the openings and closings of our conversation barriers is a practice that takes us to the roots of who we think we are. The three traffic-light slogans are reminders to keep us on track. Following this path, we learn how to transform fear into love, and to bring that love into our lives for the benefit of others.

Stepping-Stones

As an overview of this process, here are seven stepping-stones we can use to dis-identify from our mindless communication patterns:

1. Simply notice the effects that all your conversations—both external and internal—have on you. This kind of insight is mostly the product of meditation and postmeditation mindfulness. For example, in meditation we observe how our thoughts can run wild, imagining scenes, characters, and dialogues, and generating all kinds of emotional reactions. We feel our body brace with stress as we replay confrontations in our mind. Much of this internal activity may later become evident in our conversations with others. But by patiently coming back to the present moment over and over again, we can notice awareness start to penetrate our fixed patterns.

2. Get curious about your opinions and story lines instead of defending them. This practice loosens up the glue that attaches our mask to "me." Genuine curiosity is different from rhetorical questions that fortify the red zone. For instance, I might hear myself asking, *How could he do that to me?* But if I

simply stay with the primary question, "How could he do that?" I am keeping myself open, because I realize I don't actually know the answer. I am allowing there to be a gap. After all, this question might lead to a new insight. But when I add "to me," the gap closes and I find myself in a defensive posture.

3. Widen the view by noticing the overall patterns in your communication. For instance, some of us have a tendency to get excited and interrupt others. Or we may have a tendency to exaggerate, or minimize, when we replay the details of an event. Noticing these overall patterns widens the scope of our awareness. This step involves further detaching from identifying with our stories, and it strengthens our ability to change our mind.

4. Try to see the gaps in the chain of thoughts and opinions that hold your concept of "me" together. Our mind can be like a fast-moving freight train. At first our viewpoint seems solid, but when we look more closely, we can see that there are lots of gaps that we normally ignore. Any flashes we get of the "green light" are like catching sight of our own face in a mirror. For example, Fran was in the middle of entertaining her new friends with a funny but self-deprecating story about her past. Recently, in her reflections on mindfulness and communication, she had the insight that the women in her family typically use humor to put themselves down. She'd told this funny story many times before, but this time a gap opened up and Fran felt a deep sadness welling up. This sadness was a flash of the green light, the tenderhearted response to disrespecting herself. In that gap, Fran saw the contrast between the sense of dignity that she'd been gaining and the habit of using herself as the target of aggressive humor. These gaps, or interruptions, can bring us back to our senses, our heart or the openness of our mind, reminding us of who we really are. Reconnecting with here-and-now reality helps us detach from our story lines.

5. Realize that you have the power to choose. Suddenly, with this stepping-stone, we might notice, seemingly out of

nowhere, that we are open enough to feel the freedom to choose. We hear, *Wait a minute, is this what I* really *want?* For example, one of my clients described an argument she had with her partner one evening in the middle of a dark Alaskan winter, when the sun both rises and sets in the middle of the day:

> I stormed out the door, but the knee-deep snow made a mockery of my dramatic exit. I managed to plow half-way across the yard, absorbed in my raging retaliation fantasies about how I'd prove he was wrong and I was right. Then my boot got stuck and I fell forward, face-down into the wet snow. I pulled my foot out of my boot and rolled over. Wiping the cold slush from my face, I blinked at the starry sky. I felt like a child, shaking my fist at the universe, leveled by primal rage, frustration, and sadness. The reasons for my anger faded like a distant memory. I asked myself, what am I doing? It was like popping out of a dream, waking from a child's mind to adulthood. The logic of right and wrong fell apart. I felt a welling up of grief and remorse and wanted to quickly rush home to make peace. I scrambled to my feet, left my boot stuck in the snowbank and trudged back as fast as I could though my own deep footprints to the kitchen door, hoping he'd still be there.

Earlier in the book we described this turning point as a "miracle moment." This flash of green light happens when we ask the question, Do I want to be right or do I want to be happy? Suddenly a new direction opens up, and we realize we have the power to choose.

6. Question your defensive logic until you arrive at some degree of "positive doubt." With the practice of positive inter-ruptions, we begin to doubt our own confused logic. We support this with the practice of contemplation, such as in the dialogue and journal exercises offered throughout this book.

We can further our own positive doubt by noticing how closed mind depends on "toxic certainty." For example, when Lucas insisted on being "right" and chose to defend his story line rather than feel the pain of his loss, he identified with that story and ended up defending this imaginary script as "me." When the light is red, we all do this in our own unique way. Like Sarah, we can also notice how we shut down our heart out of fear by noticing how, when we're hurt or angry, the fear that we might be "wrong" gets confused with the yellow-light, core fear that there is something wrong with "me." If we try to suppress that fear, we lose the opportunity to ask the question, Who is this "self" that I'm defending, anyway? But if we open our heart, even for a moment, the game is up. Finally, instead of patching them up, we can be curious about cracks in our mask, the logic of our defensiveness. This is what happened to Paul when he began to question his own opinions about disciplining Mia. Sheila asked him, Do you want to be right or do you want to be happy? And for Paul this was a positive interruption that woke him up to the truth that he was going in the wrong direction. It led to deeper questions: Is "me" really more important than "we"? If my words inflict an emotional wound on my partner or my child, how does this benefit me? What exactly am I trying to hide from and whom am I defending in my red zone? We can actually meta-phorically jump through the gap, because every now and then, like sunlight at the end of the tunnel, we'll see the green light flashing and a sudden shift can take place.

7. Cultivate compassionate insight for yourself and others. Contemplation includes pausing and looking back to allow our new understanding to sink in. Waking up to the present moment shows us that our thoughts and opinions are insubstantial. But it also brings compassion; because we see how easily our untrained mind can be bullied by fears that seize control. When we're lost in the red zone, all our strategies to escape from this fortress of "me" only make it seem more real.

Self-Reflection Guide

These contemplations can be done in various ways: alone, as a personal conversation within ourselves in silence, in a journal, or with a trusted friend.

Opening Meditation

First, relax into the natural awakeness of your body, the natural tenderness of your heart, the natural openness of your mind. Simply rest for a few moments.

Contemplative Dialogue

Now choose one of the following contemplations, which bring the yellow-light experience of self-doubt into the green zone of unconditional friendliness.

1. *The Fear That I Am Unwelcome, or Cut Off*

Red light. Bring to mind an example of a me-first conversation that leaves the listener feeling unwelcome, unimportant, reduced from "thou" to an object.

Yellow light. Feel the sadness of being cut off in this way and the natural longing to be regarded with respect.

Green light. Remembering not to be afraid of this sadness, which is tender heart, gently open your mind to investigate the background self-doubt that is afraid you don't belong, that you have no value or that you are unwelcome in this world. See if you can pinpoint the exact moment when this fear arises, and look to find out whether it has any truth to it.

Relax and reconnect with the awakeness, tenderness, and openness of the experience of belonging.

Close by vividly imagining a we-first conversation in which both speaker and listener engage with mutual respect, keeping the channel of communication open.

2. *The Fear That I Am Unworthy*

Red light. Bring to mind an example of a seesaw conversation that leaves the listener feeling unworthy, put down, or inferior.

Yellow light. Feel the sadness of being put down in this way and the natural longing to feel valued.

Green light. Opening to this sadness, which is tender heart, gently encourage yourself to investigate the background self-doubt that is afraid you are unworthy, inadequate, or undeserving. See if you can pinpoint the exact moment when this fear arises, and look to find out whether it has any truth to it.

Relax and reconnect with the awakeness, tenderness, and openness of feeling confident in your own fundamental worthiness.

Close by vividly imagining a conversation that keeps a level playing field between speaker and listener, with a mutual sense of valuing the other person.

3. *The Fear That I Am Unforgivable*

Red light. Bring to mind an example of a blaming conversation that leaves the listener feeling unforgivable.

Yellow light. Feel the sadness of being blamed in this way and the natural longing to feel forgiven and accepted for who we are.

Green light. Making room for this sadness, which is tender heart, gently investigate the background self-doubt that is afraid you are unforgivable, fundamentally bad, and imperfect. See if you can pinpoint the exact moment when this fear arises, and look to find out whether it has any truth to it.

Relax and reconnect with the awakeness, tenderness, and openness of feeling confident in your own fundamental innocence and blamelessness.

Close by vividly imagining a difficult conversation in which the speaker can tell the truth, engage with conflict or share a painful experience while at the same time remaining openhearted to the sensitivity of the other person.

4. *The Fear That I Am Unloveable*

Red light. Bring to mind an example of an emotionally devouring conversation that leaves the listener feeling confused about the word *love* and unable to feel appreciated and genuinely cared about.

Yellow light. Feel the sadness of conditional love, and how unsafe it feels to go from being the object of love to the object of hatred. Feel the natural longing for unconditional love and joy.

Green light. Allowing this sadness, which is tender heart, to simply be there, gently open your mind to investigate the background self-doubt that is afraid that you're fundamentally unloveable, that the joy of unconditional acceptance will always be out of your reach. See if you can pinpoint the exact moment when this fear arises, and look to find out whether it has any truth to it.

Relax and reconnect with the awakeness of your sense perceptions that display the beauty of the world around you, the tenderness of your heart that feels joy and sadness and is capable of love, and the openness of your mind that is like the wonder of a young child. Rest in this unconditional friendliness.

Close by vividly imagining a conversation or an art form that expresses love without grasping or possessiveness.

5. *The Fear That I Am Powerless*

Red light. Bring to mind an example of a controlling conversation that leaves the listener feeling powerless, unable to trust your own resources.

Yellow light. Feel the sadness of losing trust in ourselves and of being controlled by someone else.

Green light. Allowing this sadness, which is tender heart, to simply be there, gently open your mind to investigate the background self-doubt that is afraid you cannot trust yourself or that the world is untrustworthy. See if you can pinpoint the exact moment when this fear arises, and look to find out whether it has any truth to it.

Relax and reconnect with the awakeness, tenderness, and openness of a basic sense of trust. Feel in partnership with the emerging information of the present moment, confident in a natural sense of power that doesn't depend on strategies.

Close by vividly imagining a conversation that resolves problems by empowering each other to feel confidence and trust in our basic sanity.

Concluding Reminders

As you conclude your self-reflection, renew your intention to practice mindful communication. If you find it helpful, bring to mind the three-light practice slogans that are easy to remember throughout the day:

- *Go with the green light.* Learn to trust openness, the natural communication of awake body, tender heart, and open mind. Cultivate a we-first approach, staying connected and keeping the communication channel open.
- *Stop when the light is red.* Refrain from conversations that

turn toxic. When the me-first barrier goes up, genuine communication stops. Learn to recognize this signal, let go, and create space, rather than pushing forward.

- *When the light is yellow, be careful.* When things don't go as planned, vulnerable feelings can trigger toxic reactions. Take advantage of this groundlessness by mindfully protecting these vulnerable feelings by creating a welcoming space, a green zone, either alone or with a trusted friend. Then apply compassionate insight to unmask the inner fears and self-doubts in our mind for what they are—merely frozen thought patterns that melt in the light of our own awareness. This is how we reconnect with the truth of our basic goodness.

Remember to be gentle, patient, and encouraging with yourself and others in this lifelong practice of transforming conversations into a path of wakefulness. There is no such thing as failure as long as we use the pain of shutting down as a reminder to be compassionate with ourselves. As my teacher said, "Now that you understand this, you cannot fall off the path. Good luck."

Notes

CHAPTER 1. STOP, GO, AND WAIT

1. Chögyam Trungpa, *The Collected Works of Chögyam Trungpa,* vol. 3 (Boston: Shambhala, 2003), 246.
2. Lee Nichol, ed., *The Essential David Bohm* (London: Routledge, 2002), 302.
3. "Beyond Vietnam," Riverside Church, New York, NY, April 4, 1967.

CHAPTER 2. THE KEY TO MINDFUL PRESENCE

1. "Sunbeams" in *The Sun,* Feb. 2007.
2. Quoted from a short film by Bill Scheffel called *Becoming A Teacher.*

CHAPTER 3. THE KEY TO MINDFUL LISTENING

1. Sakyong Mipham, *Ruling Your World: Ancient Strategies for Modern Life* (New York: Morgan Road Books, 2005), 73.

CHAPTER 4. THE KEY TO MINDFUL SPEECH

1. Izzeldin Abuelaish, *I Shall Not Hate: A Gaza Doctor's Journey on the Road to Peace and Human Dignity* (Toronto: Random House Canada, 2010), xv.

CHAPTER 6. THE KEY TO MINDFUL RESPONSES

1. Chögyam Trungpa, *The Collected Works of Chögyam Trungpa,* vol. 3 (Boston: Shambhala, 2003), 246.

2. Chögyam Trungpa, *Glimpses of Abhidharma: From a Seminar on Buddhist Psychology* (Boston: Shambhala, 2001), 95.

3. Associated Press, April 22, 2011.

Glossary

alone-together. Unconditional friendliness is supported by bringing inner solitude, or mindfulness, into our relationships. This describes a friendliness toward self that rebalances the habit of using the other person to meet our needs. Instead, we are able to appreciate other people as they are.

awake body. The innate human capacity to pay attention to our sense perceptions and the environment in the present moment, as well as to the energetic sensations in our body. Part of the **natural communication system.** See also **open mind; tender heart.**

bardo. A term from buddhist psychology that describes the interval of confusion, or gap, between one set of reference points and another. See also **yellow light.**

contemplative dialogue. A conversation that opens to new information and ideas, supported by a specific agreement to follow guidelines for mindful conversation.

enmeshment. The false intimacy of the relationship cocoon created by using another person to escape our aloneness. Because we haven't made friends with ourselves, we project our needs on the other, pulling the other person in and then pushing them away when we need space. See also **heartless-mind; mindless-heart; relationship cocoon.**

exaggerating. A red-light signal that shows us how we deceive ourselves and others in conversations, indicating that we are spinning our story by inflating certain details at the expense of others.

false self. A mistaken identity, or mask, that arises from a hidden core fear that there is something wrong with who we are. This core fear is covered up with closed communication patterns and is exposed when things don't go as planned. See also **yellow light; secondary reactions.**

four confidences of mindful communication. Seasons in the cycle of relationship and in conversations: mindful presence (winter), mindful listening (spring), mindful speech (summer), and mindful responses to differences (autumn).

four progressive stages of compassionate activity. Levels of skillful responses that naturally occur when we meet situations with awake body, tender heart, and open mind: pacifying, enriching, magnetizing, and cutting through obstacles.

four stages of heartlessness. The progressive conversations in which aggression escalates: complaint/criticism, divisiveness, blame, and retaliation.

green light. Symbol for openness, using the three gifts of awake body, tender heart, and open mind in communication with whatever is going on in the present moment.

green-light emotions. The "we-first" emotional intelligence of our natural communication system, or tender heart. Examples are compassion, courage, kindness. Because these emotions originate from openness, they are interdependent and do not harm relationships.

green zone. An emotionally safe situation that welcomes sensitive yellow-light feelings with compassionate insight. Examples include mindfulness meditation, writing in a journal, and engaging in a green-light conversation. Being selflessly present for others is the third and final stage of the path of mindful communication.

green-zone friend. Someone who shares the intention to practice mindful communication.

heartless-mind. A red-light communication pattern that bypasses tender heart and uses logic to justify harming others. See also **four stages of heartlessness.**

in-between zone. The period between being open and being closed in our communication; an opportunity to relate to our background anxiety, hidden fears, and mistaken core beliefs. See also **bardo; yellow light.**

justification. A red-light signal that insists on substituting a fictional story line for reality in order to support a toxic emotional reaction. See also **toxic certainty.**

magic moments. Those occasions when for no reason we shift abruptly from a closed to an open mind. See also **positive interruptions.**

me-first. A red-light communication style that is created by the belief that our personal survival depends on competing with others. See also **heartless-mind; mindless-heart.**

mindless-heart. A red-light communication pattern that replaces the natural boundaries of common sense with emotional or sentimental story lines that justify turning our power over to others to avoid abandonment.

minimizing. A red-light signal that shows us subtle ways we deceive ourselves and others in conversations, indicating that we are editing out important details of our experience, silencing our own truth.

mindfulness. The mind's natural capacity to remember what we are doing in the present moment. This power can weaken with neglect when we practice mindlessness, or can be strengthened with training in mindfulness meditation.

natural communication system. Our inborn gifts of awake body, tender heart, and open mind that inform us about the present moment. See also **green light.**

open mind. The innate human capacity to penetrate our own misunderstandings; to be honest, curious, and insightful; to let go of our preconceived ideas and opinions. Part of the **natural communication system.** See also **awake body; tender heart.**

openness. The centerless awareness of the present moment, our natural communication system. This awareness has three qualities: awake body, tender heart, and open mind. See also **green light; awake body; tender heart; open mind; natural communication system.**

positive doubt. When it's right to be wrong. Allowing the wisdom of "not knowing" (open mind) to interrupt the toxic certainty of our convictions.

positive interruptions. A practice of mindful communication that changes the value of interruptions from negative (not wanting to interrupt a person) to positive: allowing the "green light" or natural communication system to replace mindless habits. See also **positive doubt.**

pursuer/distancer cycle. A relationship cocoon pattern in which one partner follows a script of "mindless heart," pursuing intimacy by ignoring boundaries, while the other follows a script of "heartless-mind," creating distance for the relationship through aggression.

red light. Symbol for communication being closed.

red-light emotions. The "me-first" reactions that arise from our defensive barriers. These emotions are produced by story lines, therefore they are qualified by dualistic thinking. They include craving, hatred, paranoia, arrogance. Their characteristic is that they always cause harm at some point, either to ourselves or to others. See also **heartless-mind; mindless-heart; secondary reactions.**

red-light signals. Patterns in our conversations that indicate our communication is closed. Examples include minimizing, exaggerating, putting others down, and giving our power away.

relationship cocoon. A false stability in relationship that is achieved by both partners making an unspoken agreement to remain mindless. See also **pursuer/distancer cycle.**

secondary reactions. Learned behaviors and core beliefs that cut us off from our natural communication system. They are passed on through mindless communication patterns. See also **red-light emotions.**

seesaw pattern. A red-light signal that compares ourselves to others using praise and criticism to inflate our own importance at the expense of others. This can also happen in reverse, putting ourselves down and inflating the value of others.

selflessness. When we listen openly to the present moment our responses are not determined by personal needs alone but by the needs of the relationship or the situation.

stages of the path of mindful communication. Three stages in the process of "letting our fences down" outlined by Chögyam Trungpa and applied to the path of mindful communication practice: making friends with ourselves, disciplined patience with others, and selflessness.

surfing the wave of coincidence. A practice of playfully being open to spontaneous messages from our environment and responding appropriately.

tender heart. The raw emotional energy of open communication, which is unconditionally friendly and is naturally "we-first." Also referred to as green-light emotions. Part of the **natural communication system.** See also **awake body; open mind.**

touch-and-go practice. The activity of our natural communication system: awake body allows experience to be what it is; tender heart touches the quality of our experience, feeling what we feel; and open mind is letting go.

toxic certainty. Self-righteous opinions that divert our attention from tenderhearted empathy. See also **heartless-mind.**

toxic niceness. A mindless-heart pattern that sacrifices power and truth in order to avoid conflict and criticism at any cost. When aggression builds, it is expressed indirectly and dishonestly.

unconditional friendliness. A we-first approach to relationship that is based upon accepting ourselves and others as we are. "Unconditional" allows the flowing quality of our everyday experience and "friendliness" is the ability to feel joy when we're touched by the beauty of what we experience.

we-first. The view of open communication that we are interdependent with others and that our personal survival depends upon respecting and remaining connected to each other. See also **selflessness; openness; green light.**

yellow light. Symbol for the period in between open and closed communication.

yellow-light emotions. Fear-based feelings such as disappointment, embarrassment, shame, irritation, hurt, and a general background anxiety. They are caused by self-doubts, mistaken core beliefs that we are unlovable, unforgivable, unworthy or powerless. When we don't relate to these feelings, they cause us to hide behind a defensive barrier. Relating to them with clarity and compassion is how we gain confidence that our human nature is basically good.

About the Author

Susan Gillis Chapman grew up in Vancouver, British Columbia, and was educated at the Convent of the Sacred Heart. She received her BA at the University of British Columbia and an MA in Buddhist and Western Psychology at Naropa Institute (now Naropa University). She spent ten years working in the field of domestic violence, as program director for Boulder County Safehouse, offering counseling for battered women and their children, and as clinical director of Tongass Community Counseling Center, before opening her private practice as a marital and family therapist.

In 1997, Susan and her husband, Jerry, participated in a Buddhist three-year retreat at Gampo Abbey in Nova Scotia. Susan was invited by Pema Chödrön to stay on to lead the retreat program for another six years. Susan presently works as a part time consultant and lecturer, teaching workshops in mindful communication and is a senior teacher in the Shambhala community.